Pass the CHSPE:

California High School Proficiency Study Guide

Copyright © 2021 by Complete Test Preparation Inc. ALL RIGHTS RESERVED.

No part of this book may be reproduced or transferred in any form or by any means, graphic, electronic, or mechanical, including photocopying, recording, web distribution, taping, or by any information storage retrieval system, without the written permission of the author.

Notice: Complete Test Preparation Inc. makes every reasonable effort to obtain from reliable sources accurate, complete, and timely information about the tests covered in this book. Nevertheless, changes can be made in the tests or the administration of the tests at any time and Complete Test Preparation Inc. makes no representation or warranty, either expressed or implied as to the accuracy, timeliness, or completeness of the information contained in this book. Complete Test Preparation Inc. make no representations or warranties of any kind, express or implied, about the completeness, accuracy, reliability, suitability or availability with respect to the information contained in this document for any purpose. Any reliance you place on such information is therefore strictly at your own risk.

The author(s) shall not be liable for any loss incurred as a consequence of the use and application, directly or indirectly, of any information presented in this work. Sold with the understanding, the author is not engaged in rendering professional services or advice. If advice or expert assistance is required, the services of a competent professional should be sought.

The company, product and service names used in this publication are for identification purposes only. All trademarks and registered trademarks are the property of their respective owners. Complete Test Preparation Inc. is not affiliate with any educational institution.

Complete Test Preparation Inc. is not affiliated with, or endorsed by any official testing organization. All organizational and test names are trademarks of their respective owners.

We strongly recommend that students check with exam providers for up-to-date information regarding test content.

Please note that CHSPE is administered by the California Department of Education, which was not involved in the production of, and does not endorse, this product.

ISBN-13: 9781927358559

Version 8 Updated July 2021

About Complete Test Preparation Inc.

The Complete Test Preparation Team has been publishing high quality study materials since 2005. Over one million students visit our websites every year, and thousands of students, teachers and parents all over the world (over 100 countries) have purchased our teaching materials, curriculum, study guides and practice tests.

Complete Test Preparation Inc. is committed to providing students with the best study materials and practice tests available on the market. Members of our team combine years of teaching experience, with experienced writers and editors, all with advanced degrees.

https://www.test-preparation.ca

Feedback

We welcome your feedback. Email us at feedback@test-preparation.ca with your comments and suggestions. We carefully review all suggestions and often incorporate reader suggestions into upcoming versions. As a Print on Demand Publisher, we update our products frequently.

https://www.facebook.com/CompleteTestPreparation/

https://www.youtube.com/user/MrTestPreparation

https://www.instagram.com/test.preparation/

Contents

8 Getting Started
How this study guide is organized 9
The CHSPE Study Plan 9
Making a Study Schedule 10

15 Reading
Self-Assessment 18
Answer Key 29
Help with Reading Comprehension 33
Main Idea and Supporting Details 36
Drawing Inferences And Conclusions 40
Meaning From Context 44
Vocabulary Self-Assessment 47
Answer Key 53
Help with Building your Vocabulary 55

58 How to Write an Essay
Formulating A Thesis 68
Common Essay Mistakes - Example 1 71
Common Essay Mistakes - Example 2 73
Writing Concisely 75

78 Language Arts
Self-Assessment 79
Answer Key 90
English Grammar and Punctuation Tutorials 93
Capitalization 93
Punctuation 95
Hyphens 96
Apostrophes 98
Commas 99
Quotation Marks 101
English Grammar Multiple Choice 103
Common English Usage Mistakes 119
Subject Verb Agreement 127

134 MATHEMATICS

Self-Assessment	138
Answer Key	147
Basic math Video Tutorials	151
Fraction Tips, Tricks and Shortcuts	151
Decimal Tips, Tricks and Shortcuts	157
Converting Decimals to Fractions	157
Percent Tips, Tricks and Shortcuts	158
Exponents – a Quick Tutorial	160
How to Solve Word Problems	165
Types of Word Problems	168
Algebraic Equations	177
Ratios	179
Basic Geometry	183
Pythagorean Geometry	188
Scale drawings	190
Quadrilaterals	192

196 PRACTICE TEST QUESTIONS SET 1

Answer Key	252

274 PRACTICE TEST QUESTIONS SET 2

Answer Key	327

348 CONCLUSION

350 ONLINE RESOURCES

Getting Started

Congratulations! By deciding to take the California High School Proficiency Exam (CHSPE), you have taken the first step toward a great future! Of course, there is no point in taking this important examination unless you intend to do your best to earn the highest grade you possibly can. That means getting yourself organized and discovering the best approaches, methods and strategies to master the material. Yes, that will require real effort and dedication,, but if you are willing to focus your energy and devote the study time necessary, before you know it you will be on you way to a brighter future.

We know that taking on a new endeavour can be scary, and it is easy to feel unsure of where to begin. That's where we come in. This study guide is designed to help you improve your test-taking skills, show you a few tricks of the trade and increase both your competency and confidence.

The California High School Proficiency Exam

The CHSPE exam has three modules, English Language Arts and Math. The English Language Arts consists of English grammar and usage, vocabulary and an essay. The Math module contains basic High School math.

While we seek to make our guide as comprehensive as possible, note that like all entrance exams, the CHSPE Exam might be adjusted at some future point. New material might be added, or content that is no longer relevant or applicable might be removed. It is always a good idea to give the materials you receive when you register to take the CHSPE a careful review.

How This Study Guide is Organized

This study guide is divided into three sections. The first section, Self-Assessments, which will help you recognize your areas of strength and weaknesses. This will be a boon when it comes to managing your study time most efficiently; there is not much point of focusing on material you have already got firmly under control. Instead, taking the self-assessments will show you where that time could be much better spent. In this area you will begin with a few questions to evaluate quickly your understanding of material that is likely to appear on the CHSPE. If you do poorly in certain areas, simply work carefully through those sections in the tutorials and then try the self-assessment again.

The second section, Tutorials, offers information in each of the content areas, as well as strategies to help you master that material. The tutorials are not intended to be a complete course, but cover general principles. If you find that you do not understand the tutorials, it is recommended that you seek out additional instruction.

Third, we offer two sets of practice test questions, similar to those on the CHSPE Exam. Again, we cover all modules, so make sure to check with your school!

The CHSPE Study Plan

Now that you have made the decision to take the CHSPE, it is time to get started. Before you do another thing, you will need to figure out a plan of attack. The best study tip is to start early! The longer the time period you devote to regular study practice, the likelier that you will retain the material and access it quickly. If you thought that 1x20 is the same as 2x10, guess what? It really is not, when it comes to study time. Reviewing material for just an hour per day over the course of 20 days is far better than studying for two hours a day for only 10 days. The more often you revisit a particular piece of information, the better you will know it. Not only will your grasp and understanding be better, but your ability to reach into your brain and quickly and efficiently pull out the tidbit you need, will be greatly enhanced as well.

The great Chinese scholar and philosopher Confucius believed that true knowledge could be defined as knowing what you know and what you do not know. The first step in preparing for the CHSPE Exam is to assess your strengths and weaknesses. You may already have an idea of what you know and what you do not know, but evaluating yourself using our Self- Assessment modules for each of the three areas, Math, English and Reading Comprehension, will clarify the details.

Making a Study Schedule

To make your study time the most productive, you will need to develop a study plan. The purpose of the plan is to organize all the bits of pieces of information in such a way that you will not feel overwhelmed. Rome was not built in a day, and learning everything you will need to know to pass the CHSPE Exam is going to take time, too. Arranging the material you need to learn into manageable chunks is the best way to go. Each study session should make you feel as though you have accomplished your goal, or at least are a little closer, and your goal is simply to learn what you planned to learn during that particular session. Try to organize the content in such a way that each study session builds on previous ones. That way, you will retain the information, be better able to access it, and review the previous bits and pieces at the same time.

Self-assessment

The Best Study Tip! The best study tip is to start early!

The longer you study regularly, the more you will retain and 'learn' the material. Studying for 1 hour per day for 20 days is far better than studying for 2 hours for 10 days.

What don't you know?

The first step is to assess your strengths and weaknesses. You may already have an idea of where your weaknesses are, or you can take our Self-assessment modules for each of the areas, Math, English, Science and Reading Comprehension.

Exam Component	**Rate from 1 to 5**
English / Language Arts	
Vocabulary	
Grammar & Usage	
Punctuation	
Capitalization	
Essay Writing	
Reading Comprehension	
Math	
Algebra	
Ratio and Probability	
Percent, Decimal, Fractions	
Geometry	

Making a Study Schedule

The key to a successful study plan is to divide the material you need to learn into manageable size and learn it, while at the same time reviewing the material that you already know.

Using the table above, any scores of three or below, mean you need to spend time learning, reviewing and practicing this subject area. A score of four means you need to review the material, but you don't have to spend time re-learning. A score of five and you are OK with just an occasional review before the exam.

A score of zero or one means you really do need to work on this and you should allocate the most time and give it the highest priority. Some students prefer a 5-day plan and others a 10-day plan. It also depends on how much time you have until the exam.

Here is an example of a 5-day plan based on an example from the table above:

Vocabulary: 1   Study 1 hour everyday – review on last day
Fractions: 3   Study 1 hour for 2 days then ½ hour and then review
Algebra: 4   Review every second day
Grammar & Usage: 2 Study 1 hour on the first day – then ½ hour everyday
Reading Comprehension: 5   Review for ½ hour every other day
Geometry: 5 Review for ½ hour every other day

Using this example, geometry and reading comprehension are good and only need occasional review. Algebra is good and needs 'some' review. Fractions need a bit of work, grammar and usage needs a lot of work and vocabulary is very weak and need most time. Based on this, here is a sample study plan:

Day	Subject	Time
Monday		
Study	Vocabulary	1 hour
Study	Grammar & Usage	1 hour
	½ hour break	
Study	Fractions	1 hour
Review	Algebra	½ hour
Tuesday		
Study	Vocabulary	1 hour
Study	Grammar & Usage	½ hour
	½ hour break	

	Study	Fractions	½ hour
	Review	Algebra	½ hour
	Review	Geometry	½ hour
Wednesday			
	Study	Vocabulary	1 hour
	Study	Grammar & Usage	½ hour
		½ hour break	
	Study	Fractions	½ hour
	Review	Geometry	½ hour
Thursday			
	Study	Vocabulary	½ hour
	Study	Grammar & Usage	½ hour
	Review	Fractions	½ hour
		½ hour break	
	Review	Geometry	½ hour
	Review	Algebra	½ hour
Friday			
	Review	Vocabulary	½ hour
	Review	Grammar & Usage	½ hour
	Review	Fractions	½ hour
		½ hour break	
	Review	Algebra	½ hour
	Review	Grammar & Usage	½ hour

Using this example, adapt the study plan to your own schedule. This schedule assumes 2 ½ - 3 hours available to study everyday for a 5 day period.

First, write out what you need to study and how much. Next figure out how many days you have before the test. Note, do NOT study on the last day before the test. On the last day before the test, you won't learn anything and will probably only confuse yourself.

Make a table with the days before the test and the number of hours you have available to study each day. We suggest working with 1 hour and ½ hour time slots.

Start filling in the blanks, with the subjects you need to study the most getting the most time and the most regular time slots (i.e. everyday) and the subjects that you know getting the least time (e.g. ½ hour every other day, or every 3rd day).

Tips for making a schedule

Once you make a schedule, stick with it! Make your study sessions reasonable. If you make a study schedule and don't stick with it, you set yourself up for failure. Instead, schedule study sessions that are a bit shorter and set yourself up for success! Make sure your study sessions are do-able. Studying is hard work but after you pass, you can party and take a break!

Schedule breaks. Breaks are just as important as study time. Work out a rotation of studying and breaks that works for you.

Build up study time. If you find it hard to sit still and study for 1 hour straight through, build up to it. Start with 20 minutes, and then take a break. Once you get used to 20-minute study sessions, increase the time to 30 minutes. Gradually work you way up to 1 hour.

40 minutes to 1 hour is optimal. Studying for longer than this is tiring and not productive. Studying for shorter isn't long enough to be productive.

Studying Math. Studying Math is different from studying other subjects because you use a different part of your brain. The best way to study math is to practice everyday. This will train your mind to think in a mathematical way. If you miss a day or days, the mathematical mind-set is gone and you have to start all over again to build it up.

Study and practice math everyday for at least 5 days before the exam.

ONLINE STUDY SCHEDULE CREATOR

https://www.test-preparation.ca/make-a-chspe-study-schedule/

Reading

This section contains a self-assessment and reading tutorial. The Tutorials are designed to familiarize general principles and the self-assessment contains general questions similar to the reading questions likely to be on the CHSPE exam, but are not intended to be identical to the exam questions. The tutorials are not designed to be a complete reading course, and it is assumed that students have some familiarity with reading comprehension questions. If you do not understand parts of the tutorial, or find the tutorial difficult, it is recommended that you seek out additional instruction.

Note that these questions are for skill practice only.

Tour of the CHSPE Reading Content

The CHSPE reading section has 54 reading questions which includes reading comprehension and vocabulary. Below is a more detailed list of the types of reading questions that generally appear on the CHSPE.

- Drawing logical conclusions

- Identify the author's intent to persuade, inform, or

entertain.

- Make predictions

- Analyze and evaluate the use of text structure to solve problems or identify sequences

- Identify the characteristics of a passage types (narrative, expository, technical, persuasive).

- Give the definition of a word from context

- Find specific information from a different types of communication (memo, posted notice etc.)

The questions below are not the same as you will find on the CHSPE - that would be too easy! And nobody knows what the questions will be and they change all the time. Mostly the changes consist of substituting new questions for old, but the changes can be new question formats or styles, changes to the number of questions in each section, changes to the time limits for each section and combining sections. Below are general reading questions that cover the same areas as the CHSPE. So, while the format and exact wording of the questions may differ slightly, and change from year to year, if you can answer the questions below, you will have no problem with the reading section of the CHSPE.

READING SELF-ASSESSMENT

The purpose of the self-assessment is:

- Identify your strengths and weaknesses.

- Develop your personalized study plan (above)

- Get accustomed to the CHSPE format

- Extra practice – the self-assessments are almost a full 3rd practice test!

- Provide a baseline score for preparing your study schedule.

Since this is a Self-assessment, and depending on how confident you are with Reading Comprehension, timing is optional. The CHSPE has 35 reading questions. The self-assessment has 12 questions, so allow about 15 minutes to complete this assessment.

Once complete, use the table below to assess your understanding of the content, and prepare your study schedule described in chapter 1.

80% - 100%	Excellent – you have mastered the content
60 – 79%	Good. You have a working knowledge. Even though you can just pass this section, you may want to review the Tutorials and do some extra practice to see if you can improve your mark.
40% - 59%	Below Average. You do not understand the reading comprehension problems. Review the tutorials, and retake this quiz again in a few days, before proceeding to the rest of the Practice Test Questions.
Less than 40%	Poor. You have a very limited understanding of the reading comprehension problems. Please review the Tutorials, and retake this quiz again in a few days, before proceeding to the Practice Test Questions.

READING COMPREHENSION SELF-ASSESSMENT

	A	B	C	D
1	○	○	○	○
2	○	○	○	○
3	○	○	○	○
4	○	○	○	○
5	○	○	○	○
6	○	○	○	○
7	○	○	○	○
8	○	○	○	○
9	○	○	○	○
10	○	○	○	○
11	○	○	○	○
12	○	○	○	○
13	○	○	○	○
14	○	○	○	○
15	○	○	○	○
16	○	○	○	○

VOCABULARY SELF-ASSESSMENT

	A	B	C	D	E		A	B	C	D	E
1	○	○	○	○	○	21	○	○	○	○	○
2	○	○	○	○	○	22	○	○	○	○	○
3	○	○	○	○	○	23	○	○	○	○	○
4	○	○	○	○	○	24	○	○	○	○	○
5	○	○	○	○	○	25	○	○	○	○	○
6	○	○	○	○	○						
7	○	○	○	○	○						
8	○	○	○	○	○						
9	○	○	○	○	○						
10	○	○	○	○	○						
11	○	○	○	○	○						
12	○	○	○	○	○						
13	○	○	○	○	○						
14	○	○	○	○	○						
15	○	○	○	○	○						
16	○	○	○	○	○						
17	○	○	○	○	○						
18	○	○	○	○	○						
19	○	○	○	○	○						
20	○	○	○	○	○						

Directions: The following questions are based on several reading passages. A series of questions follow each passage. Read each passage carefully, and then answer the questions based on it. You may reread the passage as often as you wish. When you have finished answering the questions based on one passage, go right onto the next passage. Choose the best answer based on the information given and implied.

Questions 1 – 4 refer to the following passage.

Passage 1 - Who Was Anne Frank?

You may have heard mention of the word Holocaust in your History or English classes. The Holocaust took place from 1939-1945. It was an attempt by the Nazi party to purify the human race, by eliminating Jews, Gypsies, Catholics, homosexuals and others they deemed inferior to their "perfect" Aryan race. The Nazis used Concentration Camps, which were sometimes used as Death Camps, to exterminate the people they held in the camps. The saddest fact about the Holocaust was the over one million children under the age of sixteen died in a Nazi concentration camp. Just a few weeks before World War II was over, Anne Frank was one of those children to die.

Before the Nazi party began its persecution of the Jews, Anne Frank had a happy live. She was born in June of 1929. In June of 1942, for her 13th birthday, she was given a simple present which would go onto impact the lives of millions of people around the world. That gift was a small red diary that she called Kitty. This diary was to become Anne's most treasured possession when she and her family hid from the Nazi's in a secret annex above her father's office building in Amsterdam.

For 25 months, Anne, her sister Margot, her parents, another family, and an elderly Jewish dentist hid from the Nazis in this tiny annex. They were never permitted to go outside, and their food and supplies were brought to them by Miep Gies and her husband, who did not believe in the Nazi persecution of the Jews. It was a very difficult life for young Anne and she used Kitty as an outlet to describe her life in hiding.

After 2 years, Anne and her family were betrayed and arrested by the Nazis. To this day, nobody is exactly sure who betrayed the Frank family and the other annex residents. Anne, her mother, and her sister were separated from Otto Frank, Anne's father. Then, Anne and Margot were separated from their mother. In March of 1945, Margot Frank died of starvation in a Concentration Camp. A few days later, at the age of 15, Anne Frank died of typhus. Of all the people who hid in the Annex, only Otto Frank survived the Holocaust.

Otto Frank returned to the Annex after World War II. It was there that he found Kitty, filled with Anne's thoughts and feelings about being a persecuted Jewish girl. Otto Frank had Anne's diary published in 1947 and it has remained continuously in print ever since. Today, the diary has been published in over 55 languages and more than 24 million copies have been sold around the world. The Diary of Anne Frank tells the story of a brave young woman who tried to see the good in all people.

1. From the context clues in the passage, what does annex mean?

    a. Attic

    b. Bedroom

    c. Basement

    d. Kitchen

2. Why do you think Anne's diary has been published in 55 languages?

    a. So everyone could understand it.

    b. So people around the world could learn more about the horrors of the Holocaust.

    c. Because Anne was Jewish but hid in Amsterdam and died in Germany.

    d. Because Otto Frank spoke many languages.

3. From the description of Anne and Margot's deaths in the passage, what can we assume typhus is?

    a. The same as starving to death.

    b. An infection the Germans gave to Anne.

    c. A disease Anne caught in the concentration camp.

    d. Poison gas used by the Germans to kill Anne.

4. In the third paragraph, what does outlet mean?

    a. A place to plug things into the wall

    b. A store where Miep bought cheap supplies for the Frank family

    c. A hiding space similar to an Annex

    d. A place where Anne could express her private thoughts.

Questions 5 – 8 refer to the following passage.

Passage 2 - Was Dr. Seuss a Real Doctor?

A favorite author for over 100 years, Theodor Seuss Geisel was born on March 2, 1902. Today, we celebrate the birthday of the famous "Dr. Seuss" by hosting Read Across America events throughout the March. School children around the country celebrate the "Doctor's" birthday by making hats, giving presentations and holding read aloud circles featuring some of Dr. Seuss' most famous books.

But who was Dr. Seuss? Did he go to medical school? Where was his office? You may be surprised to know that Theodor Seuss Geisel was not a medical doctor at all. He took on the nickname Dr. Seuss when he became a noted children's book author. He earned the nickname because people said his books were "as good as medicine." All these years later, his nickname has lasted and he is known as Dr. Seuss all across the world.

Think back to when you were a young child. Did you ever want to try "green eggs and ham?" Did you try to "Hop on Pop?" Do you remember learning about the environment from a creature called The Lorax? Of course, you must recall one of Seuss' most famous characters; that green Grinch who stole Christmas. These stories were all written by Dr. Seuss and featured his signature rhyming words and letters. They also featured made up words to enhance his rhyme scheme and even though many of his characters were made up, they sure seem real to us today.

And what of his "signature" book, The Cat in the Hat? You must remember that cat and Thing One and Thing Two from your childhood. Did you know that in the early 1950's there was a growing concern in America that children were not becoming avid readers? This was, book publishers thought, because children found books dull and uninteresting. An intelligent publisher sent Dr. Seuss a book of words that he thought all children should learn as young readers. Dr. Seuss wrote his famous story The Cat in the Hat, using those words. We can see, over the decades, just how much influence his writing has had on very young children. That is why we celebrate this doctor's birthday each March.

5. What does the word "avid" mean in the last paragraph?

    a. Good

    b. Interested

    c. Slow

    d. Fast

6. What can we infer from the statement " His books were like medicine?"

    a. His books made people feel better

    b. His books were in doctor's office waiting rooms

    c. His books took away fevers

    d. His books left a funny taste in readers' mouths.

7. Why is the publisher in the last paragraph called "intelligent?"

    a. a. The publisher knew how to read.

    b. The publisher knew that kids did not like to read.

    c. The publisher knew Dr. Seuss would be able to create a book that sold well.

    d. The publisher knew that Dr. Seuss would be able to write a book that would get young children interested in reading.

8. The theme of this passage is

    a. Dr. Seuss was not a doctor.

    b. Dr. Seuss influenced the lives of generations of young children.

    c. Dr. Seuss wrote rhyming books.

    d. Dr. Seuss' birthday is a good day to read a book.

Questions 9 - 12 refer to the following passage.

Keeping Tropical Fish

Keeping tropical fish at home or in your office used to be very popular. Today, interest has declined, but it remains as rewarding and relaxing a hobby as ever. Ask any tropical fish hobbyist, and you will hear how soothing and relaxing watching colorful fish live their lives in the aquarium. If you are considering keeping tropical fish as pets, here is a list of the basic equipment you will need.

A filter is essential for keeping your aquarium clean and your fish alive and healthy. There are different types and sizes of filters and the right size for you depends on the size of the aquarium and the level of stocking. Generally, you need a filter with a 3 to 5 times turn over rate per hour. This means that the water in the tank should go through the filter about 3 to 5 times per hour.

Most tropical fish do well in water temperatures ranging between $24°C$ and $26°C$, though each has its own ideal water temperature. A heater with a thermostat is necessary to regulate the water temperature. Some heaters are submersible and others are not, so check carefully before you buy.

Lights are also necessary, and come in a large variety of types, strengths and sizes. A light source is necessary for plants in the tank to photosynthesize and give the tank a more attractive appearance. Even if you plan to use plastic plants, the fish still require light, although here you can use a lower strength light source.

A hood is necessary to keep dust, dirt and unwanted materials out of the tank. Sometimes the hood can also help prevent evaporation. Another requirement is aquarium gravel. This will improve the aesthetics of the aquarium and is necessary if you plan to have real plants.

9. What is the general tone of this article?

    a. Formal
    b. Informal
    c. Technical
    d. Opinion

10. Which of the following cannot be inferred?

   a. Gravel is good for aquarium plants.

   b. Fewer people have aquariums in their office than at home.

   c. The larger the tank, the larger the filter required.

   d. None of the above.

11. What evidence does the author provide to support their claim that aquarium lights are necessary?

   a. Plants require light.

   b. Fish and plants require light.

   c. The author does not provide evidence for this statement.

   d. Aquarium lights make the aquarium more attractive.

12. Which of the following is an opinion?

   a. Filter with a 3 to 5 times turn over rate per hour are required.

   b. Aquarium gravel improves the aesthetics of the aquarium.

   c. An aquarium hood keeps dust, dirt and unwanted materials out of the tank.

   d. Each type of tropical fish has its own ideal water temperature.

Questions 13 - 16 refer to the following passage.

The Civil War

The Civil War began on April 12, 1861. The first shots of the Civil War were fired in Fort Sumter, South Carolina. Note that even though more American lives were lost in the Civil

War than in any other war, not one person died on that first day. The war began because eleven Southern states seceded from the Union and tried to start their own government, The Confederate States of America.

Why did the states secede? The issue of slavery was a primary cause of the Civil War. The eleven southern states relied heavily on their slaves to foster their farming and plantation lifestyles. The northern states, many of whom had already abolished slavery, did not think that the southern states should have slaves. The north wanted to free all the slaves and President Lincoln's goal was to both end slavery and preserve the Union. He had Congress declare war on the Confederacy on April 14, 1862. For four long, blood soaked years, the North and South fought.

From 1861 to mid 1863, it seemed as if the South would win this war. However, on July 1, 1863, an epic three day battle was waged on a field in Gettysburg, Pennsylvania. Gettysburg is remembered for being the bloodiest battle in American history. At the end of the three days, the North turned the tide of the war in their favor. The North then went on to dominate the South for the remainder of the war. A famous episode is General Sherman's "March to The Sea," where he famously led the Union Army through Georgia and the Carolinas, burning and destroying everything in their path.
In 1865, the Union army invaded and captured the Confederate capital of Richmond Virginia. Robert E. Lee, leader of the Confederacy surrendered to General Ulysses S. Grant, leader of the Union forces, on April 9, 1865. The Civil War was over and the Union was preserved.

13. What does secede mean?

    a. To break away from

    b. To accomplish

    c. To join

    d. To lose

14. Which of the following statements summarizes a FACT from the passage?

    a. Congress declared war and then the Battle of Fort Sumter began.

    b. Congress declared war after shots were fired at Fort Sumter.

    c. President Lincoln was pro slavery

    d. President Lincoln was at Fort Sumter with Congress

15. Which event finally led the Confederacy to surrender?

    a. The battle of Gettysburg

    b. The battle of Bull Run

    c. The invasion of the confederate capital of Richmond

    d. Sherman's March to the Sea

16. What does the word abolish as used in this passage mean?

    a. To ban

    b. To polish

    c. To support

    d. To destroy

Answer Key

1. A
We know that an annex is like an attic because the text states the annex was above Otto Frank's building.

Choice B is incorrect because an office building doesn't have bedrooms. Choice C is incorrect because a basement would be below the office building. Choice D is incorrect because there would not be a kitchen in an office building.

2. B
The diary has been published in 55 languages so people all over the world can learn about Anne. That is why the passage says it has been continuously in print.

Choice A is incorrect because it is too vague. Choice C is incorrect because it was published after Anne died and she did not write in all three languages. Choice D is incorrect because the passage does not give us any information about what languages Otto Frank spoke.

3. C
Use the process of elimination to figure this out.

Choice A cannot be the correct answer because otherwise the passage would have simply said that Anne and Margot both died of starvation. Choices B and D cannot be correct because if the Germans had done something specifically to murder Anne, the passage would have stated that directly. By the process of elimination, choice C has to be the correct answer.

4. D
We can figure this out using context clues. The paragraph is talking about Anne's diary and so, outlet in this instance is a place where Anne can pour her feelings.

Choice A is incorrect answer. That is the literal meaning of the word outlet and the passage is using the figurative meaning. Choice B is incorrect because that is the secondary literal meaning of the word outlet, as in an outlet mall. Again, we are looking for figurative meaning. Choice C is incorrect because there are no clues in the text to support that answer.

5. B
When someone is avid about something that means they are highly interested in the subject. The context clues are dull and boring, because they define the opposite of avid.

6. A
The author is using a simile to compare the books to medicine. Medicine is what you take when you want to feel better. They are suggesting that if a person wants to feel good, they should read Dr. Seuss' books.

Choice B is incorrect because there is no mention of a doctor's office. Choice C is incorrect because it is using the literal meaning of medicine and the author is using medicine in a figurative way. Choice D is incorrect because it makes no sense. We know not to eat books.

7. D
The publisher is described as intelligent because he knew to get in touch with a famous author to develop a book that children would be interested in reading.

Choice A is incorrect because we can assume that all book publishers must know how to read. Choice B is incorrect because it says in the article that more than one publisher was concerned about whether or not children liked to read. Choice C is incorrect because there is no mention in the article about how well The Cat in the Hat sold when it was first published.

8. B
The passage describes in detail how Dr. Seuss had a great effect on the lives of children through his writing. It names several of his books, tells how he helped children become avid readers and explains his style of writing.

Choice A is incorrect because that is just one single fact about the passage. Choice C is incorrect because that is just one single fact about the passage. Choice D is incorrect because that is just one single fact about the passage. Again, choice B is correct because it encompasses ALL the facts in the passage, not just one single fact.

9. B
The general tone is informal.

10. B
The statement, "Fewer people have aquariums in their office than at home," cannot be inferred from this article.

11. B
Light is necessary for the fish and plants.

12. B
The following statement is an opinion, " Aquarium gravel improves the aesthetics of the aquarium."

13. A
Secede means to break away from because the 11 states wanted to leave the United States and form their own country.

Choice B is incorrect because the states were not accomplishing anything. Choice C is incorrect because the states were trying to leave the USA not join it. Choice D is incorrect because the states seceded before they lost the war.

14. B
Look at the dates in the passage. The shots were fired on April 12 and Congress declared war on April 14.

Choice C is incorrect because the passage states that Lincoln was against slavery. Choice D is incorrect because it never mentions who was or was not at Fort Sumter.

15. C
The passage states that Lee surrendered to Grant after the capture of the capital of the Confederacy, which is Richmond.

Choice A is incorrect because the war continued for 2 years after Gettysburg. Choice B is incorrect because that battle is not mentioned in the passage. Choice D is incorrect because the capture of the capital occurred after the march to the sea.

16. A

When the passage said that the North had *abolished* slavery, it implies that slaves were no longer allowed in the North. In essence slavery was banned.

Choice B makes no sense relative to the context of the passage. Choice C is incorrect because we know the North was fighting slavery, not for it. Choice D is incorrect because slavery is not a tangible thing that can be destroyed. It is a practice that had to be outlawed or banned.

Help with Reading Comprehension

At first sight, reading comprehension tests look challenging especially if you are given long essays to answer only two to three questions. While reading, you might notice your attention wandering, or you may feel sleepy. Do not be discouraged because there are various tactics and long-range strategies that make comprehending even long, boring essays easier.

Your friends before your foes. It is always best to start with passages with familiar subjects rather than those with unfamiliar ones. This approach applies the same logic as tackling easy questions before hard ones. Skip passages that do not interest you and leave them for later.

Don't use 'special' reading techniques. This is not the time for speed-reading or anything like that – just plain ordinary reading – not too slow and not too fast.

Read through the entire passage and the questions before you do anything. Many students try reading the questions first and then looking for answers in the passage thinking this approach is more efficient. What these students do not realize is that it is often hard to navigate in unfamiliar roads. If you do not familiarize yourself with the passage first, looking for answers become not only time-consuming but also dangerous because you might miss the context of the answer you are looking for. If you read the questions first you will only confuse yourself and lose valuable time.

Familiarize yourself with reading comprehension questions. If you are familiar with the common types of reading questions, you are able to take note of important parts of the passage, saving time. There are six major kinds of reading questions.

- **Main Idea**- Questions that ask for the central thought or significance of the passage.

- **Specific Details** - Questions that asks for explicitly stated ideas.

- **Drawing Inferences** - Questions that ask for a logical extension of statements.

- **Tone or Attitude** - Questions that test your ability to sense the emotional state of the author.

- **Context Meaning** – Questions that ask for the meaning of a word depending on the context.

- **Technique** – Questions that ask for the method of organization or the writing style of the author.

Read. Read. Read. The best preparation for reading comprehension tests is always to read, read and read. If you are not used to reading lengthy passages, you will probably lose concentration. Increase your attention span by making a habit out of reading. Read everyday and increase the time slowly each day.

Reading Comprehension tests become less daunting when you have trained yourself to read and understand fast. Always remember that it is easier to understand passages you are interested in. Do not read through passages hastily. Make mental notes of ideas you may be asked.

Reading Strategy

When facing the reading comprehension section of a standardized test, you need a strategy to be successful. You want to keep several steps in mind:

- **First, make a note of the time and the number of sections.** Time your work accordingly. Typically, four to five minutes per section is sufficient. Second, read the directions for each selection thoroughly before beginning (and listen carefully to any additional verbal instructions, as they will often clarify obscure or confusing written guidelines). You must know exactly how to do what you're about to do!

- **Now you're ready to begin reading the selection.** Read the passage carefully, noting significant characters or events on scrap paper or underlining on the test sheet. Many students find making a basic list in the margins helpful. Quickly jot down or underline one-word summaries of characters, notable happenings, numbers, or key ideas. This will help retain information and focus wandering thoughts. Remember, however, that your goal is to find the information that answers the questions. Even if you find the passage interesting, stay on track.

- **Now read the question and all the choices.** Now you have read the passage, have a general idea of the main ideas, and have marked the important points. Read the question and all the choices. Never choose an answer without reading them all! Questions are often designed to confuse – stay focussed and clear. Usually the answer choices will focus on one or two facts or inferences from the passage. Keep these clear in your mind.

- **Search for the answer.** With a very general idea of what the different choices are, go back to the passage and scan for the relevant information. Watch for big words, unusual or unique words. These make your job easier as you can scan the text for the particular word.

- **Mark the Answer.** Now you have the key information the question is looking for. Go back to the question, quickly scan the choices and mark the correct one.

Typically, there will be several questions dealing with facts from the selection, a couple more inference questions dealing with logical consequences of those facts, and periodically an application-oriented question surfaces to force you to make connections with what you already know. Some students prefer to answer the questions as listed, and feel classifying the question and then ordering is wasting precious time. Other students prefer to answer the different types of questions in order of how easy or difficult they are. The choice is yours and do whatever works for you. If you want to try answering in order of difficulty, here is a recommended order, answer fact questions first; they're easily found within the passage. Tackle inference problems next, after re-reading the question(s) as many times as you need to. Application or 'best guess' questions usually take the longest, so, save them for last.

Use the practice tests to try out both ways of answering and see what works for you.

For more help with reading comprehension, see Multiple Choice Secrets at www.multiple-choice.ca

Main Idea and Supporting Details

Identifying the main idea, topic and supporting details in a passage can feel like an overwhelming task. The passages used for standardized tests can be boring and seem difficult - Test writers don't use interesting passages or ones that talk about things most people are familiar with. Despite these obstacles, all passages and paragraphs will have the information you need to answer the questions.

The topic of a passage or paragraph is its subject. It's the general idea and can be summed up in a word or short phrase. Sometimes, there is a short description of the passage if it's taken from a longer work. Make sure you read the description as it might state the topic of the passage. If not, read the passage and ask yourself, "Who, or what is this about?" For example:

> Over the years, school uniforms have been hotly debated. Arguments are made that students have the right to show individuality and express themselves by choosing their own clothes. However, this brings up social and academic issues. Some kids cannot afford to wear the clothes they like and might be bullied by the "better dressed" students. With attention drawn to clothes and the individual, students will lose focus on class work and the reason they are in school. School uniforms should be mandatory.

Ask: What is this paragraph about?

Topic: school uniforms

Once you have the topic, it's easier to find the main idea. The main idea is a specific statement telling what the writer wants you to know. Writers usually state the main idea as a thesis statement. If you're looking for the main idea of a single paragraph, the main idea is called the topic sentence and will probably be the first or last sentence. If you're looking for the main idea of an entire passage, look for the thesis statement in either the first or last paragraph. The main idea is usually restated in the conclusion. To find the main idea of a passage or paragraph, follow these steps:

1. Find the topic.

2. Ask yourself, "What point is the author trying to make about the topic?"

3. Create your own sentence summarizing the author's point.

4. Look in the text for the sentence closest in meaning to yours.

Look at the example paragraph again. It's already established that the topic of the paragraph is school uniforms. What is the main idea/topic sentence?

Ask: "What point is the author trying to make about school uniforms?"

Summary: Students should wear school uniforms.

Topic sentence: School uniforms should be mandatory.

Main Idea: School uniforms should be mandatory.

Each paragraph offers supporting details to explain the main idea. The details could be facts or reasons, but they will always answer a question about the main idea. What? Where? Why? When? How? How much/many? Look at the example paragraph again. You'll notice that more than one sentence answers a question about the main idea. These are the supporting details.

Main Idea: School uniforms should be mandatory.

Ask: Why? Some kids cannot afford to wear clothes they like and could be bullied by the "better dressed" kids. Supporting Detail

With attention drawn to clothes and the individual, Students will lose focus on class work and the reason they are in school. Supporting Detail

What if the author doesn't state the main idea in a topic sentence? The passage will have an implied main idea. It's not as difficult to find as it might seem. Paragraphs are always organized around ideas. To find an implied main idea, you need to know the topic and then find the relationship between the supporting details. Ask yourself, "What is the point the author is making about the relationship between the details?"

> Cocoa is what makes chocolate good for you. Chocolate comes in many varieties. These delectable flavors include milk chocolate, dark chocolate, semi-sweet, and white chocolate.

Ask: What is this paragraph about?

Topic: Chocolate

Ask: What? Where? Why? When? How? How much/many?

Supporting details: Chocolate is good for you because it is made of cocoa, Chocolate is delicious, Chocolate comes in different delicious flavors

Ask: What is the relationship between the details and what is the author's point?

Main Idea: Chocolate is good because it is healthy and it tastes good.

Testing Tips for Main Idea Questions

1. Skim the questions – not the answer choices - before reading the passage.

2. Questions about main idea might use the words "theme," "generalization," or "purpose."

3. Save questions about the main idea for last. Questions can often be found in order in the passage.

3. Underline topic sentences in the passage. Most tests allow you to write in your test booklet.

4. Answer the question in your own words before looking at the answer choices. Then match your answer with an answer choice.

5. Cross out incorrect answer choices immediately to prevent confusion.

6. If two of the answer choices mean the same thing but use different words, they are BOTH incorrect.

7. If a question asks about the whole passage, cross out the answer choices that apply to only part of it.

8. If only part of the information is correct, that answer choice is incorrect.

9. An answer choice that is too broad is incorrect. All information needs to be backed up by the passage.

10. Answer choices with extreme wording are usually incorrect.

Drawing Inferences And Conclusions

Video Tutorial

https://www.test-preparation.ca/making-inferences-and-drawing-conclusions-video-tutorial/

Drawing inferences and making conclusions happens all the time. In fact, you probably do it every time you read—sometimes without even realizing it! For example, remember the first time that you saw the movie "The Lion King." When you meet Scar for the first time, he is trapping a helpless mouse with his sharp claws preparing to eat it. When you see this action you guess that Scar is going to be a bad character in the movie. Nothing appeared to tell you this. No caption came across the bottom of the screen that said "Bad Guy." No red arrow pointed to Scar and said "Evil Lion." No, you made an inference about his character based on the context clue you were given. You do the same thing when you read!

When you draw an inference or make a conclusion you are doing the same thing, you are making an educated guess based on the hints the author gives you. We call these hints "context clues." Scar trapping the innocent mouse is the context clue about Scar's character.

Usually you are making inferences and drawing conclusions the entire time that you are reading. Whether you realize it or not, you are constantly making educated guesses based on context clues. Think about a time you were reading a book and something happened that you were expecting to happen. You're not psychic! Actually, you were picking up on the context clues and making inferences about what was going to happen next!

Let's try an easy example. Read the following sentences and answer the questions at the end of the passage.

Shelly really likes to help people. She loves her job because she gets to help people every single day. However, Shelly has to work long hours and she can get called in the middle of the night for emergencies. She wears a white lab coat at work and usually she carries a stethoscope.

What is most likely Shelly's job?

    a. Musician

    b. Lawyer

    c. Doctor

    d. Teacher

This probably seemed easy. Drawing inferences isn't always this simple, but it is the same basic principle. How did you know Shelly was a doctor? She helps people, she works long hours, she wears a white lab coat, and she gets called in for emergencies at night. Context Clues! Nowhere in the paragraph did it say Shelly was a doctor, but you were able to draw that conclusion based on the information provided in the paragraph. This is how it's done!

There is a catch, though. Remember that when you draw inferences based on reading, you should only use the information given to you by the author. Sometimes it is easy for us to make conclusions based on knowledge that is already in our mind—but that can lead you to drawing an incorrect inference. For example, let's pretend there is a bully at your school named Brent. Now let's say you read a story and the main character's name is Brent. You could NOT infer that the character in the story is a bully just because his name is Brent. You should only use the information given to you by the author to avoid drawing the wrong conclusion.

Let's try another example. Read the passage below, and answer the question.

Social media is an extremely popular new form of connecting and communicating over the internet. Since Facebook's original launch in 2004, millions of people have joined in the social media craze. In fact, it is estimated that almost 75% of all internet users aged 18 and older use some form of social media. Facebook started at Harvard University as a way to get students connected. However, it quickly grew into a worldwide phenomenon and today, the founder of Facebook, Mark Zuckerberg has an estimated net worth of 28.5 billion dollars.

Facebook is not the only social media platform, though. Other sites such as Twitter, Instagram, and Snapchat have since been invented and are quickly becoming just as popular! Many social media users actually use more than one type of social media. Furthermore, most social media sites have created mobile apps that allow people to connect via social media virtually anywhere in the world!

What likeliest reason that other social media sites like Twitter and Instagram were created?

> a. Professors at Harvard University made it a class project.
>
> b. Facebook was extremely popular and other people thought they could also be successful by designing social media sites.
>
> c. Facebook was not connecting enough people.
>
> d. Mark Zuckerberg paid people to invent new social media sites because he wanted lots of competition.

Here, the correct answer is B. Facebook was extremely popular and other people thought they could also be successful by designing social media sites. How do we know this? What are the context clues? Take a look at the first paragraph. What do we know based on this paragraph? Well, one sentence refers to Facebook's original launch. This suggests that Facebook was one of the first social media sites. In addition, we know that the founder of Facebook has been extremely successful and is worth billions of dollars. From this we can infer that other people wanted to imitate Facebook's idea and become just as successful as Mark Zuckerberg.

Let's go through the other answers. If you chose A, it might be because Facebook started at Harvard University, so you drew the conclusion that all other social media sites were also started at Harvard University. However, there is no mention of class projects, professors, or students designing social media. So there doesn't seem to be enough support for choice A.

If you chose C, you might have been drawing your own conclusions based on outside information. Maybe none of your friends are on Facebook, so you made an inference that Facebook didn't connect enough people, so more sites were invented. Or maybe you think the people who connect on Facebook are too old, so you don't think Facebook connects enough people your age. This might be true, but remember inferences should be drawn from the information the author gives you!

If you chose D, you might be using the information that Mark Zuckerberg is worth over 28 billion dollars. It would be easy for him to pay others to design new sites, but remember, you need to use context clues! He is very wealthy, but that statement was giving you information about how successful Facebook was—not suggesting that he paid others to design more sites!

So remember, drawing inferences and conclusions is simply about using the information you are given to make an educated guess. You do this every single day so don't let this concept scare you. Look for the context clues, make sure they support your claim, and you'll be able to make accurate inferences and conclusions!

Meaning From Context

Often in reading comprehension questions, you are asked for the definition of a word, which you have to infer from the surrounding text, called "meaning in context." Here are a few examples with step-by-step solutions, and a few tips and tricks to answering meaning from context questions.

There are literally thousands and thousands of words in the English language. It is impossible for us to know what every single one of them means, but we also don't have time to Google a definition every time we read a word we don't understand! Even the smartest person in the world comes across words they don't know, but luckily we can use context clues to help us determine what things actually mean.

Context clues are really just little hints that can help us determine the meaning of words or phrases and honestly, the easiest way to learn how to use context clues is to practice!

Let's start with a few basic examples.

> In some countries many people are not given access to schools, teachers, or books. In these countries, people might be illiterate.

You might not know what the word illiterate means, but let's use the clues in the sentence to help us. If people are not given access to schools, teachers, or books, what might happen? They probably don't learn what we learned in school so they might not know some of the things that we learned from our teachers! Illiterate actually means "unable to read or write." This makes sense based on the context clues!

Let's work through another example.

> We have so much technology today! So much technology that many people have started using tablets and computers to read ebooks instead of paper books! In fact, some of these people actually think that reading paper books is archaic!

Let's look for the context clues. Well, what do we know from this paragraph? We have a lot of technology and sometimes people read ebooks instead of paper books. From this we can draw the conclusion that ebooks are beginning to replace paper books because ebooks are newer and better. So if ebooks are newer and better, it must mean that paper books are older. Archaic actually means "very old or old-fashioned," which again we determined from the context clues.

Let's see if you can try a few on your own now.

> Cody noticed the strawberries in his refrigerator were old and moldy, so he abstained and threw them away.

What does abstained most likely mean?

> a. chose not to consume
>
> b. washed
>
> c. shared
>
> d. cut into pieces

The correct answer here is A. The context clues told you the strawberries were old and moldy and told you that Cody did something and then threw them away. If the strawberries were moldy, and Cody abstained, it makes sense that he didn't eat them—which is choice A.

You may have chosen answer B. If the strawberries were old and moldy, Cody could have washed them. But use ALL of the context clues. After he abstained, he threw them away. Why would Cody wash them and then throw them away? That doesn't make sense! In addition, why would he share them if they were old and moldy? Finally, I suppose Cody could have cut them into pieces, but why would he need to do that before throwing them away? It doesn't make as much sense, so choice A is the correct answer!

Let's do one more.

Scott had a disdain for Lily ever since she lied to their boss and got him fired.

a. Compassion
b. Hate
c. Remorse
d. Money

The correct answer is B. Scott was fired because Lily lied. Can you imagine if this happened to you? I think you would have some pretty strong feelings just like Scott!

It's simple! By understanding the context, you can determine the meaning of even the hardest of words!

VOCABULARY SELF-ASSESSMENT

1. Choose the noun that means, self evident or clear obvious truth.

    a. Truism

    b. Catharsis

    c. Libertine

    d. Tractable

2. Choose the best definition for: virago

    a. A loud domineering woman

    b. A quiet woman

    c. A load domineering Man

    d. A quiet man

3. When Joe broke his _____ in a skiing accident, his entire leg was in a cast.

    a. Ankle

    b. Humerus

    c. Wrist

    d. Femur

4. Select another word for the underlined word in the sentence below.

At first I thought she was very rude and boorish, but when I talked to her again she was very <u>genteel.</u>

    a. Chivalrous

    b. Hilarious

    c. Civilized

    d. Governance

5. Choose an adjective that means corrupted, impure.

    a. Adulterate
    b. Harbor
    c. Infuriate
    d. Inculcate

6. Select another word for the underlined word in the sentence below.

Her business success showed that she was very <u>shrewd</u>.

    a. Slow
    b. Astute
    c. Ignorant
    d. Heinous

7. Choose an adjective that means, beyond what is obvious or evident.

    a. Ulterior
    b. Sybarite
    c. Torsion
    d. Trenchant

8. Choose a noun that means, homeless child or stray.

    a. Elegy
    b. Waif
    c. Martyr
    d. Palaver

9. Select another word for the underlined word in the sentence below.

His inheritance was very large - a <u>princely</u> sum!

    a. Minor
    b. Tolerable
    c. Large
    d. Pittance

10. What is the best definition of deprecate?

    a. Approve
    b. Indifference
    c. Disapprove
    d. None of the above

11. Choose the best definition for succor.

    a. To suck on
    b. To hate
    c. To like
    d. Give help or assistance

12. Select the synonym of conspicuous.

    a. Important
    b. Prominent
    c. Beautiful
    d. Convincing

13. Select the noun that means eagerness and enthusiasm.

    a. Alacrity

    b. Happiness

    c. Donator

    d. Marital

14. After Lisa's aunt had her tenth child, Lisa found that she had more than twenty _____.

    a. Uncles

    b. Friends

    c. Stepsisters

    d. Cousins

15. Select the word that means benevolence.

    a. Happiness

    b. Courage

    c. Kindness

    d. Loyalty

16. Select the verb that means, to make less severe.

    a. Suspense

    b. Alleviate

    c. Ingrate

    d. Action

17. What is the name of one who gives a gift or who gives money to a charity organization?

    a. Captain
    b. Benefactor
    c. Source
    d. Teacher

18. What is another word for subordinate, or person of lesser rank or authority?

    a. Palliate
    b. Plebeian
    c. Underling
    d. Expiate

19. Choose the best definition of specious.

    a. Logical
    b. Illogical
    c. Emotional
    d. 2 species

20. Choose the best definition of proscribe.

    a. Welcome
    b. Write a prescription
    c. Condemn
    d. Give a diagnosis

21. When Craig's dog was struck by a car, he rushed his pet to the _____.

    a. Emergency room
    b. Doctor
    c. Veterinarian
    d. Podiatrist

22. Choose the best definition of the underlined word. She never made a mistake - her performance was always impeccable.

    a. Charming
    b. Flattering
    c. Perfect
    d. Impervious

23. Select the synonym of boisterous.

    a. Loud
    b. Soft
    c. Gentle
    d. Warm

24. Select the adjective that means hidden, secret, disguised.

    a. Accustomed
    b. Covert
    c. Hide
    d. Carriage

25. Select the verb that means straightforward, open and sincere.

    a. Lawful
    b. Candid
    c. True
    d. Lawful

Answer Key

1. A
Truism: n. self-evident or clear, obvious, truth.

2. A
Virago: Given to undue belligerence or ill manner at the slightest provocation; a shrew, a termagant.

3. D
Femur: n. The bone of the thigh or upper hind limb, articulating at the hip and the knee.

4. C
Genteel: Polite and well-mannered. Stylish or elegant. Aristocratic

5. A
Adulterate: v. To render (something) poorer in quality by adding another substance, typically an inferior one.

6. B
Shrewd: showing clever resourcefulness in practical matters, artful, tricky or cunning, astute, streetwise, knowledgeable

7. A
Ulterior: adj. beyond what is obvious or evident.

8. B
Waif: n. homeless child or stray.

9. C
Princely: In the manner of a royal prince's conduct; large or grand.

10. C
Deprecate: v. To belittle or express disapproval of.

11. D
Succor: v. Aid, assistance or relief given to one in distress; ministration.

12. B
Conspicuous: adj. Standing out so as to be clearly visible..

13. A
Alacrity: adj. Eagerness; liveliness; enthusiasm.

14. D
Cousins

15. C
Benevolent: adj. Well meaning and kindly.

16. B
Alleviate: v. To make less severe, as a pain or difficulty.

17. B
Benefactor: n. Somebody who gives one a gift. Usually refers to someone who gives money to a charity or another form of organization.

18. C
Underling: n. subordinate of lesser rank or authority.

19. B
Specious: adj. Seemingly well-reasoned or factual, but actually fallacious or insincere; strongly held but false.

20. C
Proscribe: v. Denounce or condemn.

21. C
Veterinarian: n. A person qualified to treat diseased or injured animals.

22. C
Impeccable: adj. Perfect, without faults, flaws or errors.

23. A
Boisterous: adj. Noisy, energetic, and cheerful; rowdy.

24. B
Covert: adj. Partially hidden, disguised, secret, surreptitious.

25. B
Candid: adj. Straightforward, open and sincere.

HELP WITH BUILDING YOUR VOCABULARY

Vocabulary tests can be daunting when you think of the enormous number of words that might come up in the exam. As the exam date draws near, your anxiety will grow because you know that no matter how many words you memorize, chances are, you will still remember so few. Here are some tips which you can use to hurdle the big words that may come up in your exam without having to open the dictionary and memorize all the words known to humankind.

Build up and tear apart the big words. Big words, like many other things, are composed of small parts. Some words are made up of many other words. A man who lifts weights for example, is a weight lifter. Words are also made up of word parts called prefixes, suffixes and roots. Often times, we can see the relationship of different words through these parts.

A person who is skilled with both hands is ambidextrous. A word with double meaning is ambiguous. A person with two conflicting emotions is ambivalent. Two words with synonymous meanings often have the same root. Bio, a root word derived from Latin is used in words like biography meaning to write about a person's life, and biology meaning the study of living organisms.

- **Words with double meanings.** Did you know that the word husband not only means a man married to a woman, but also thrift or frugality? Sometimes, words have double meanings. The dictionary meaning, or the denotation of a word is sometimes different from the way we use it or its connotation.

- **Read widely, read deeply and read daily.** The best way to expand your vocabulary is to familiarize yourself with as many words as possible through reading. By reading, you are able to remember words in a proper context and thus, remember its meaning or at the very least, its use. Reading widely would help you get acquainted with words you may never use every day. This is the best strategy without doubt. However, if you are studying for an exam next week, or even tomorrow, it isn't much help! Below you will find a range of different ways to learn new words quickly and efficiently.

- **Remember.** Always remember that big words are easy to understand when divided into smaller parts, and the smaller words will often have several other meanings aside from the one you already know. Below is an extensive list of root or stem words, followed by one hundred questions to help you learn word stems.

Here are suggested effective ways to help you improve your vocabulary.

Be Committed To Learning New Words. To improve your vocabulary you need to make a commitment to learn new words. Commit to learning at least a word or two a day. You can also get new words by reading books, poems, stories, plays and magazines. Expose yourself to more language to increase the number of new words that you learn.

- **Learn Practical Vocabulary**. As much as possible, learn vocabulary that is associated with what you do and that you can use regularly. For example learn words related to your profession or hobby. Learn as much vocabulary as you can in your favorite subjects.

- **Use New Words Frequently**. When you learn a new word start using it and do so frequently. Repeat it when you are alone and try to use the word as often as you can with people you talk to. You can also use flashcards to practice new words that you learn.

- **Learn the Proper Usage.** If you do not understand the proper usage, look it up and make sure you have it right.

- **Use a Dictionary**. When reading textbooks, novels or assigned readings, keep the dictionary nearby. Also learn how to use online dictionaries and WORD dictionary. When you come across a new word, check for its meaning. If you cannot do so immediately, then you should write it down and check it when possible. This will help you understand what the word means and exactly how best to use it.

- **Learn Word Roots, Prefixes and Suffixes.** English words are usually derived from suffixes, prefixes and roots, which come from Latin, French or Greek. Learning the root or origin of a word helps you easily understand the meaning of the word and other words that are derived from the root. Generally, if you learn the meaning of one root word, you will understand two or three words. See our List of Stem Words below. This is a great two-for-one strategy. Most prefixes, suffixes, roots and stems are used in two, three or more words, so if you know the root, prefix or suffix, you can guess the meaning of many words.

- **Synonyms and Antonyms.** Most words in the English language have two or three (at least) synonyms and antonyms. For example, "big," in the most common usage, has about seventy-five synonyms and an equal number of antonyms. Understanding the relationships between these words and how they all fit together gives your brain a framework, which makes them easier to learn, remember and recall.

- **Use Flash Cards.** Flash cards are one of the best ways to memorize things. They can be used anywhere and anytime, so you can make use of odd free moments waiting for the bus or waiting in line. Make your own or buy commercially prepared flash cards, and keep them with you all the time.

- **Make word lists.** Learning vocabulary, like learning many things, requires repetition. Keep a new words journal in a separate section or separate notebook. Add any words that you look up in the dictionary, as well as from word lists. Review your word lists regularly.

Photocopying or printing off word lists from the Internet or handouts is not the same. Actually writing out the word and a few notes on the definition is an important process for imprinting the word in your brain. Writing out the word and definition in your New Word Journal, forces you to concentrate and focus on the new word. Hitting PRINT or pushing the button on the photocopier does not do the same thing.

Notice the verbs in bold in the examples above. They are encircling the subjects of each sentence rather than following them. This is inverse word order.

How to Write an Essay

Writing an essay can be a difficult process, especially under time constraints in an exam. Here are three simple steps to help you to write a solid, well thought out essay:

1. Brainstorm potential themes and general ideas for your essay.

2. Outline your essay step by step, including subheadings for ease of understanding.

3. Write your essay carefully being aware of proper grammar and sentence structure.

Brainstorming

You should first spend some time thinking about the general subject of the essay. If the essay is asking a question, you must make sure to answer this fully in your essay. You may find it helpful to highlight key words in your assignment or use a simple spider diagram to jot down key ideas.

Example

Read the following information and complete

the following assignment:

Joseph Conrad is a Polish author who lived in England for most of his life and wrote a prolific amount of English literature. Much of his work was completed during the height of the British Empire's colonial imperialism.

Assignment: What impact has Joseph Conrad had on modern society? Present your point of view on the matter and support it with evidence. Your evidence may include reasoning, logic, examples from readings, your own experience, and observations.

Joseph Conrad

> **Background?** sailor, adventure, Polish immigrant, Youth, Nostromo, Heart of Darkness
> **Themes in his works?** ivory, silver trading, colonialism, corruption, greed
> **Thoughts?** descent into madness, nature of evil

Outlining (or planning)

An outline or plan is critical to organize your thoughts and ideas fully and logically. There are many ways to do this; the easiest is to write down the following headings:

1. Title
2. Introduction
3. Body
4. Conclusion

You should then jot down key ideas and themes that fit logically under the appropriate heading. This plan is now the backbone of your essay.

Tip: Even if you are not required to produce an outline or plan for the assignment, you should always leave it with your essay in the exam booklet or the back of the assignment paper. Simply draw a line across it and write 'plan' or 'outline'. This demonstrates to the reader the approach you use in formulating and finally writing your essay.

Writing the essay

Your introduction is what will help the reader to decide whether they want to read the rest of your essay. The introduction also introduces the subject matter and allows you to provide a general background to the reader. The first sentence is very important and you should avoid starting the essay with openers such as 'I will be comparing...'

Example

> Born as Józef Teodor Konrad Korzeniowski on December 3rd, 1857, Joseph Conrad led an adventurous life. As a Polish immigrant, Conrad never quite fit into England where he spent most of his adult life. As a younger man, Conrad made a living off sailing voyages. These swashbuckling experiences soon had him writing tales of the high seas such as one of his first works, Youth. While his early, adventurous work was of high quality, Conrad is best remembered for shedding light on the exploitative side of colonialism. Age and experience led him to start writing about (and challenging) the darker side of the imperial way of thinking. Conrad's work has forever soured words such as colonialism and imperialism.

In the main, or body of your essay, you should always be yourself and be original.

- Avoid using clichés.
- Be aware of your tone.
- Consider the language that you use. Avoid jargon and slang. Use clear prose and imagery.
- Your writing should always flow; remember to use transitions, especially between paragraphs. Read aloud in your head to make sure a paragraph sounds right.
- Always try to use a new paragraph for new ideas.

EXAMPLE

Conrad's written fiction focused on themes such as greed and power. He portrayed these two concepts as purveyors of evil. Greed and power may take on different guises, but the end result would always be the same.

Perhaps his most famous piece, The Heart of Darkness, is about the descent of an English ivory trader, Mr. Kurtz, into madness. We are taken up a river resembling the Congo by a narrator, Marlow, who is sent to retrieve Mr. Kurtz. Marlow eventually finds that Kurtz has been diluted by power and greed, the two things that spurred on colonialism in Africa. Kurtz has taken charge of a large tribe of natives (that he brutalizes) and has been hoarding ivory for himself.

Much of Conrad's later work was cut from the same vein as The Heart of Darkness. His crowning achievement is considered Nostromo where he takes an idealistic hero and corrupts him with colonial greed. Only this time the greed is for silver, not ivory.

Conrad's work resonates with readers partly because it was semi-autobiographical. Where his experience sailing the high seas helped bring his adventure stories to light, likewise did his experience witnessing atrocities in Africa reverberate through his writing.

The conclusion is your last chance to impress your reader and brings your entire essay to a logical close. You may want to link your conclusion back to your introduction or provide some closing statements. Do not panic if you cannot close your essay off completely. Few subjects offer closure.

Your conclusion should always be consistent with the rest of the essay and you should never introduce a new idea in your conclusion. It is also important to remember that a weak conclusion can diminish the impact of a good essay.

EXAMPLE

> *In sum, Joseph Conrad's life experiences and masterful writing left a lasting impact on the image of progress and what it meant to "move forward." He brought to light the cost in human lives that was required for Europe to continue mining natural resources from foreign lands. Joseph Conrad had a permanent impact on imperial culture, and colonial brutality has been on the decline ever since his work was published.*

PRESENTATION

Poor grammar and punctuation can ruin an otherwise good essay. You should always follow any requirements about the presentation of your essay, such as word count. You should also make sure that your writing is legible. Always allow time for one final read-through before submission.

Tip: If you are able to, write with double spacing. If you make a mistake, you can cross it out and write the correction on the blank line above.

Some final points to think about for writing a solid, well thought out essay:

- A good essay will contain a strong focus.
- There is no set essay structure but you can use sub-headings for better readability.
- Avoid particularly sensitive or controversial material. If you must write about something controversial, always make sure to include counter arguments.
- Your essay may have little to do with the subject itself; it is about what you make of the subject.

- Your essay can include examples from your readings, experience, studies or observations.

- Spend time doing practice essays and looking at sample essays beforehand.

ANOTHER EXAMPLE

Lets look at another example using the three steps required to write a good essay:

1. **Brainstorming**
2. **Outlining**
3. **Writing**

Using a second essay, we can now explore these three steps in further detail.

BRAINSTORMING

EXAMPLE

> *Think about the information that follows and the assignment below.*
>
> *People often quote the last two lines of Robert Frost's "The Road not Taken" as being metaphorical for success. The line's read "I took the one less traveled by, / And that has made all the difference" (19, 20).*
>
> *Assignment: Analyze and interpret this poem. Consider the poem's place in Modernist culture and Robert Frost's personal experiences. Read in between the lines and identify the more complex aspects/themes of this poem. Outline and complete an essay that challenges the point of view presented above, that the poem is synonymous with success. Provide evidence backed up by logic, experience, research, and/or examples from the poem.*

The assignment and key words that appear in the brief above are being highlighted. This confirms that the essay is not asking a specific question, but it is asking for discussion of the subject matter and phrases.
This is the time to take a few moments to jot down initial thoughts about the assignment. Do not worry too much about proper grammar at this point, just get all your thoughts down on paper:

"The Road Not Taken" by Robert Frost

> **Background?** Modernist poetry
> **Themes?** Life decisions, regret, fate, the unknown future
> **Thoughts?** The diverging roads are symbolic, the sigh at end signifies regret, life has many twists and turns, you can end in a drastically different situation later after a simple decision now

OUTLINING (OR PLANNING)

Outlining or planning is the next important stage in the process and you should always spend a few minutes writing a plan. This plan is just as important as the essay itself. You can also note how much time you may want to spend on a particular section. Make sure to assign headings to each main section of the essay and include important questions/themes you want to address.

EXAMPLE

> **1. Title**
>
> **2. Essay introduction**
> *Identify and discuss the underlying theme/s in Robert Frost's "The Road Not Taken"*
> *What was Frost's background and its applicability to understanding this poem?*
>
> **3. Essay body**
> *Quick summary of the poem*

Discuss key themes and other concepts
Discuss how these things relate to Modernism

4. Essay conclusion
Rephrase the themes of Robert Frost's poem and their place in modernist doctrine

This plan is now the outline for the essay.

WRITING THE ESSAY

The introduction is important, as it needs to introduce the reader to the essay in a way that will encourage them to continue reading. A good introduction will introduce the subject matter to a reader and point out relevant information that may be helpful to know when reading the rest of the essay.

EXAMPLE

Identify and discuss the underlying theme/s in Robert Frost's "The Road Not Taken"

Robert Frost wrote during the artistic movement after World War I known as Modernism. One purpose of modernism was to remake things in a new light, to analyze and change symptoms of societies that had plunged the European world into a grisly war. Frost's poem, "The Road Not Taken," carries with it a burden of regret that was a staple of Modernist art.

This introduction opens with what explaining about the time period of Robert Frost and real life influences to the theme of his poem, "The Road Not Taken." It contains some powerful language that will encourage the reader to continue reading and gives a solid base in understanding the remainder of the essay.

The main, or body **of the essay** is also very important:

EXAMPLE

"The Road Not Taken" was almost assuredly influenced by Robert Frost's personal life. He

was very familiar with facing difficult decisions. Frost had to make the decision to send both his sister and daughter to mental institutions. His son Carol committed suicide at the age of 38. The list of loss Frost experienced in his life goes on, but it suffices to say he was familiar with questioning the past.

With no other hints of the narrator's identity, it is best to assume that he is a man similar to Frost himself. The poem itself is about a nameless narrator reflecting on when he traveled through the autumn woods one day. He had come across a split in the road and expresses regret that he could not travel both. Each road is described as looking similar and as having equal wear but it is also mentioned one was grassier. The roads were unknown to the narrator, and shared equal possibilities in how well they may or may not be around their bends. He tells his listener with a sigh that he had made his decision and had taken "the road less traveled by" (19). Even though he had little idea which road would be better in the long run, the one he chose proved difficult.

This poem is a collection of all the insecurities and possibilities that come with even the simplest decisions. We experience the sorrow expressed by the narrator in the opening lines with every decision we make. For all the choices you make in life, there is a counterweight of choices you have not made. In a way, we are all missing half of our lives' possibilities. This realization causes a mixture of regret and nostalgia, but also stokes in us the keen awareness that missed opportunities are inevitable and regretting them is a waste of energy. We often find ourselves stuck, as the narrator is, between questioning the decisions we've made and knowing that this natural process isn't exactly productive.

> Unsolvable regret and nostalgia are things that the Modernists fought with on a regular basis. They often experimented in taking happenings of the past and reinventing them to fit a new future.

The body of the essay opens with providing a brief overview of Robert Frost's personal life and his life's relevance to the over arching theme of dealing with difficult decisions in the poem, "The Road Not Taken."

A new paragraph starts where appropriate and at the end of the discussion of Robert Frost's life, a transition moves the reader back to the start of the book (closing off this section). This also helps to move the reader towards the next discussion point.

The tone of this essay is formal, mainly because of the seriousness of the subject – regret and nostalgia plays a major role in people's lives all around the world.

For the conclusion, there will be a summary of the main discussion. While it is ideal for you to impress the reader with your writing, more importantly you need to make sure you cover all your bases and address the assignment appropriately with a closing statement about any important points you discussed in the body of your essay.

EXAMPLE

> In conclusion, Robert Frost's poem "The Road Not Taken" deals with themes of fate, regret, sorrow, and the many possibilities our decisions hold. Consider how easy it would be to upturn your life today if you made a few decisions you normally wouldn't. Frost's poem forces us to consider the twists and turns our lives take. Perhaps with a sigh, we could all think about the choices that for us have made all the difference.

This conclusion is consistent with the rest of the essay in

terms of style. There are no new ideas introduced and it has referred to the main points in the assignment title.

Finally, a full read-through is necessary before submission. It only takes a couple of minutes to read through and pick up any errors. Remember to double-space to leave room for any corrections to be made. You can also leave spacing at the end of each paragraph in case you should need to add an additional sentence or two.

Formulating A Thesis

Formulating a thesis statement can be one of the most challenging and frustrating things when writing an essay. However, it is also one of the most important things. A thesis statement summarizes your entire essay or argument into one sentence. A good thesis statement is unbiased, limited to one main idea, and has no doubts. Does it sound complicated? Well, let's un-complicate it! The best way to learn about a good thesis is to compare and contrast some bad ones.

Let's start with some informative thesis statements. Informative thesis statements don't have an opinion so they are typically easier to write. To begin with, let's look at a familiar movie.

-Aladdin is sort of a criminal, but I think he's really nice, and he falls in love with the princess and they defeat Jafar and live happily ever after.

-Aladdin is a lovable thief who falls in love with a princess and uses his wit and good heart to save a kingdom from the evil sorcerer, Jafar.

Both of these statements summarize the movie Aladdin. However, which one of these is a better thesis statement? The second one. Why? Well, let's look closer. The first statement gives a quick summary of the movie, but look at the language. That statement uses phrases like "sort of" and "I think." These don't make very good thesis statements because of their uncertainty and bias. The second statement, though, is very confident and provides just enough information to the reader. There is no room for doubt and it is quick and to the point. These are qualities of a solid thesis statement.

While the example above was simply an informative thesis, most thesis statements make a claim or argument. Let's take a look at another example that declares an opinion.

-I feel that Harry Potter is one of the greatest characters ever written because I believe he persevered and was very strong through the gravest of evils.

-Harry Potter is one of the greatest characters ever written because he consistently shows strength and perseverance through the gravest of evils.

These thesis statements are very similar. However, the second one is still better. Let's look at why. Take a look at some of the language in the first thesis statement. Are there doubts? Are there biased statements? "I feel" and "I believe" are both biased phrases. The second statement removes the biased statements and becomes a much stronger thesis.

Here are a few more tips that might help:

- A thesis statement is always a declarative statement and never a question.

    Bad: Is Harry Potter the greatest character ever written because of his strength and perseverance through the gravest of evils?

- A good thesis statement never uses "qualifiers" like might, maybe, perhaps, most likely, possibly, etc.

    Bad: Harry Potter might be the greatest character ever written because he possibly shows the most strength and perseverance through what is most likely the gravest of evils in literature.

- Thesis statements don't argue both sides of a debate.

    Bad: Harry Potter is the greatest character ever written because of his strength and perseverance through the gravest of evils, but Hermione is also the greatest character because she is incredibly smart and helps Harry defeat Voldemort.

Let's look at two more examples to clarify this even more. Look at the essay prompts and then look at the two thesis examples that follow. Determine which thesis statement is better.

Does participation in extracurricular activities in high school help students perform better academically?

    -High school students who are involved in extracurricular activities are more engaged in school which leads to better academic performances.

    -High school students who are involved in extracurricular activities are usually more engaged in school which can lead to better academic performances usually.

Number 1 is the better choice. It leaves out all the extra biased and uncertain language and makes a clear and concise argument. Let's try one more.

Should all high school teachers be required to have master's degrees before teaching?

    -High school teachers educate the future generation and should be required to have a master's degree so they are experts in teaching their subjects, even though I know many teachers who do not have master's degrees who are great at their job.

    -High school teachers educate the future generation and should be required to have a master's degree so they are experts in teaching their subjects.

The second thesis statement is better here. What is wrong with the first one? It brings in personal information by using "I" and it also argues both sides of the debate. The second is concise and states a clear opinion without any personal bias.

Writing good thesis statements takes practice so don't get discouraged if you write two or three before you find the right one for your essay! You may also need to write a few sentences that summarize your main idea and opinion before you tackle the full thesis statement. This is okay! Find what works for you! Just remember the main ideas. Your thesis should be clear and concise, it should state your opinion without any doubts, and it should be unbiased.

Common Essay Mistakes - Example 1

Whether the topic is love or action, reality television shows damage society. Viewers witness the personal struggles of strangers and they experience an outpouring of emotions in the name of entertainment. This can be dangerous on many levels. Viewers become numb to real emotions and values. Run the risk of not interpreting a dangerous situation correctly. 1 The reality show participant is also at risk because they are completely exposed. 2 The damage to both viewers and participants leads to the destruction of our healthy societal values.

Romance reality shows are dangerous to the participants and contribute to the emotional problems witnessed in society today as we set up a system built on equality and respect, shows like "The Bachelor" tear it down. 3 In front of millions of viewers every week, young women compete for a man. Twenty-five women claim to be in love with a man they just met. The man is reduced to an object they compete for. There are tears, fights, and manipulation aimed at winning the prize. 4 Imagine a young woman's reality when she returns home and faces the scrutiny of viewers who watched her unravel on television every Monday night. These women objectify themselves and have learned 5 that relationships are a combination of hysteria and competition. This does not give hope to a society based on family values and equality.

6 While incorporating the same manipulations and breakdown of relationships offered on "The Bachelor," shows like "Survivor" add another level of danger. Not only are they building a society based on lying to each other, they are competing in physical challenges that become dangerous. In the name of entertainment, these challenges become increasingly physical and are usually held in a hostile environment. The viewer's ability to determine the safety of an activity is messed up. 7 To entertain and preserve their pride, participants continue in competitions regardless of the danger level. For example, 8 participants on "Survivor" have sustained serious injuries as heart attack and burns. Societal rules are based on the safety of its citizens, not on hurting yourself for entertainment.

     Reality shows of all kinds are dangerous to participants. They damage society. 9

1. Correct sentence fragments. Who/what runs the risk? Add a subject or combine sentences. Try: "Viewers become numb to real emotions and run the risk of not interpreting a dangerous situation correctly."

2. Correct redundant phrases. Try: "The reality show participant is also at risk because they are exposed."

3. Correct run-on sentences. Decide which thoughts should be separated. Try: "Romance reality shows are dangerous to participants and contribute to the emotional problems of society today. As we support a system built on equality and respect, shows like "The Bachelor" tear it down."

4. Vary sentence structure and length. Try: "Twenty-five women claim to be in love with a man who is reduced to be the object of competition. There are tears, fights, and manipulation aimed at winning the prize."

5. Use active voice. Try: These women objectify themselves and learned that relationships are a combination of hysteria and competition.

6. Use transitions to tie paragraphs together. Try: Start the paragraph with, "Action oriented reality shows are equally as dangerous to the participants."

7. Avoid casual language/slang. Try: "The viewer's ability to determine the safety of an activity is compromised."

8. Don't address the essay. Avoid phrases like "for example" and "in conclusion." Try: "Participants on "Survivor" have sustained serious injuries as heart attack and burns.

9. Leave yourself time to write a strong conclusion! Try: Designate 3-5 minutes for writing your conclusion.

Common Essay Mistakes - Example 2

Questioning authority makes society stronger. In every aspect our society, there is an authoritative person or group making rules. There is also the group underneath them who are meant to follow. 1 This is true of our country's public schools as well as our federal government. The right to question authority at both of these levels is guaranteed by the United States Declaration of Independence. People are given the ability to question so that authority figures are kept in check 2 and will be forced to listen to the opinions of other people. Questioning authority leads to positive changes in society and preserves what is already working well.

If students never question the authority of a principal's decisions, the best interest of the student body is lost. Good things 3 may not remain in place for the students and no amendment to the rules are sought. Change requires that authority be questioned. An example of this is Silver Head Middle School in Davie, Florida. Last year, the principal felt strongly about enforcing the school's uniform policy. Some students were not bothered by this. 4 Many students felt the policy disregarded their civil rights. A petition voicing student dissatisfaction was signed and presented to the principal. He met with a student representative to discuss the petition. Compromise was reached in the form of a monthly "casual day." The students were able to promote change and peace by questioning authority.

Even at the level of federal government, our country's ultimate authority, the ability to question is the key to the harmony keeping society strong. Most government officials are elected by the public so they have the right to question their authority. 5 If there's a mandate, law, or statement that citizens aren't 6 happy with, they have recourse. Campaigning for or against a political platform and participating in the electoral process give a voice to every opinion. I think elections are very important. 7 Without this questioning and examination of society's laws, the government will represent only the voice of the authority figure. The success of our society is based on the questioning of authority. 8
    Society is strengthened by those who question authority. Dialogue is created between people with different visions and change becomes possible. At both the level of public school and of federal government, the positive effects of questioning authority can be witnessed. Whether questioning the decisions of a single principal or the motives of the federal government, it is the willingness of people to question and create change that allows society to grow. A strong society is inspired by many voices, all at different levels. 9 These voices keep society strong.

1. Write concisely. Combine the sentences to improve understanding and cut unnecessary words. Try: "In every aspect of society, there is an authority making rules and a group of people meant to follow them."

2. Avoid slang. Re-word "kept in check." Try: "People are given the ability to question so that authority figures are held accountable and will be forced to listen to the opinions of other people.

2-2. Cut unnecessary words. Try: "People are given the

ability to question so that authority figures are held accountable and will listen to other opinions."

3. Use precise language. What are "good things?" Try: "Interesting activities may not remain in place for the students and no amendment to the rules are sought."
Use correct subject-verb agreement. Be careful to identify the correct subject of your sentence. Try: "Interesting activities may not remain in place for the students and no amendment to the rules is sought."

4. Don't add information that doesn't add value to your argument. Cut: "Some students weren't bothered by this."

5. Check for parallel structure. Who has the right to question whose authority? Try: "Having voted them in, the people have the authority to question public officials."

6. Don't use contractions in academic essays. Try: "If there is a mandate, law, or statement that citizens are not happy with, they have recourse."

7. Don't use the pronoun "I" in persuasive essays. Cut opinions. Cut:"I think elections are very important."

8. Use specific examples to prove your argument. Try: Discuss a particular election in depth.

9. Cut redundant sentences. Cut: "A strong society is inspired by many voices, all at different levels."

Writing Concisely

Concise writing is direct and descriptive. The reader follows the writer's thoughts easily. If your writing is concise, a four paragraph essay is acceptable for standardized tests. It's better to write clearly about fewer ideas than to write poorly about many.

This doesn't always mean using fewer words. It means that

every word you use is important to the message. Unnecessary or repetitive information dilutes ideas and weakens your writing. The meaning of the word concise comes from the Latin, "to cut up." If it isn't necessary information, don't waste precious testing minutes writing it down.

Being redundant is a quick way to lengthen a sentence or paragraph, but it takes away your power during a timed essay. While many writers use repetition of phrases and key words to make their point, it's important to remove words that don't add value. Redundancy can confuse and lead you away from your subject when you need to write quickly. Be aware that many redundant phrases are part of our daily language and need to be cut from your essay.

For example, "bouquet of flowers" is a redundant phrase as only the word "bouquet" is necessary. Its definition includes flowers. Be especially careful with words you use to stress a point, such as "completely," "totally," and "very."

First of all, I'd like to thank my family.
Revised: First, I'd like to thank my family.

The school *introduced a new* rule.
Revised: The school introduced a rule.

I am *completely full*.
Revised: I am full.

Your glass is *totally empty*!
Revised: Your glass is empty!

Her artwork is *very unique*.
Revised: Her artwork is unique.

Other ways to cut bulk and time include avoiding phrases that have no meaning or power in your essay. Phrases like "in my opinion," "as a matter of fact," and "due to the fact that" are space and time wasters. Also, change passive verbs to active voice.

In my opinion, the paper is well written.
Revised: The paper is well written.

The book *was written* by the best students.
Revised: The best students wrote the book.

The teacher *is listening* to the students.
The teacher listens to the students.
This assigns action to the subject, shortens, and clarifies the sentence. When time is working against you, precise language is on your side.

Not only should you remove redundant phrases, whole sentences without value should be cut too. Replacing general nouns with specific ones is an effective way to accomplish this.

She screamed as the thing came closer. It was a sharp-toothed dog.
Revised: She screamed as the sharp-toothed dog came closer.

The revised sentence is precise and the paragraph is improved by combining sentences and varying sentence structure. When editing, ask yourself which thoughts should be connected and which need to be separated. Skim each paragraph as you finish writing it and cut as you go.

Leave three to four minutes for final editing. While reading, make a point to pause at every period. This allows you to "hear" sentences the way your reader will, not how you meant them to sound. This will help you find the phrases and sentences that need to be cut or combined. The result is an essay a grader will appreciate.

LANGUAGE ARTS

This section contains an English self-assessment and English tutorials. The Tutorials are designed to familiarize general principles and the self-assessment contains general questions similar to the English questions likely to be on the CHSPE exam, but are not intended to be identical to the exam questions. The tutorials are not designed to be a complete English course, and it is assumed that students have some familiarity with English. If you do not understand parts of the tutorial, or find the tutorial difficult, it is recommended that you seek out additional instruction.

Note that these questions are for skill practice only.

TOUR OF THE CHSPE ENGLISH CONTENT

The CHSPE English and Language Usage section has 48 questions. Below is a detailed list of the topics likely to appear on the CHSPE.

Language Arts

- English Grammar and Usage

- Meaning in Context (Vocabulary)

- Spelling

- Punctuation

- Capitalization

- Sentence Structure

The questions below are not the same as you will find on the CHSPE - that would be too easy! And nobody knows what the questions will be and they change all the time. Mostly, the changes consist of substituting new questions for old, but the changes also can be new question formats or styles, changes to the number of questions in each section, changes to the time limits for each section, and combining sections. So, while the format and exact wording of the questions may differ slightly, and changes from year to year, if you can answer the questions below, you will have no problem with the English section of the CHSPE.

LANGUAGE ARTS SELF-ASSESSMENT

The purpose of the self-assessment is:

- Identify your strengths and weaknesses.

- Develop your personalized study plan (above)

- Get accustomed to the CHSPE format

- Extra practice – the self-assessment is a 3rd test!
- Provide a baseline score for preparing your study schedule.

Since this is a self-assessment, and depending on how confident you are with English Grammar, timing yourself is optional. The CHSPE English and Language Usage section has 30 questions which must be answered in 40 minutes. The self-assessment has 25 questions, so allow 40 minutes to complete this assessment.

Once complete, use the table below to assess your understanding of the content and prepare your study schedule described in chapter 1.

80% - 100%	Excellent – you have mastered the content
60 – 79%	Good. You have a working knowledge. Even though you can just pass this section, you may want to review the Tutorials and do some extra practice to see if you can improve your mark.
40% - 59%	Below Average. You do not understand the content. Review the tutorials, and retake this quiz again in a few days, before proceeding to the rest of the Practice Test Questions.
Less than 40%	Poor. You have a very limited understanding. Please review the Tutorials, and retake this quiz again in a few days, before proceeding to the Practice Test Questions.

English Language Arts

	A	B	C	D	E		A	B	C	D	E
1	○	○	○	○	○	21	○	○	○	○	○
2	○	○	○	○	○	22	○	○	○	○	○
3	○	○	○	○	○	23	○	○	○	○	○
4	○	○	○	○	○	24	○	○	○	○	○
5	○	○	○	○	○	25	○	○	○	○	○
6	○	○	○	○	○						
7	○	○	○	○	○						
8	○	○	○	○	○						
9	○	○	○	○	○						
10	○	○	○	○	○						
11	○	○	○	○	○						
12	○	○	○	○	○						
13	○	○	○	○	○						
14	○	○	○	○	○						
15	○	○	○	○	○						
16	○	○	○	○	○						
17	○	○	○	○	○						
18	○	○	○	○	○						
19	○	○	○	○	○						
20	○	○	○	○	○						

Part 1 - Punctuation

1. Ted and Janice <u>who had been friends for years went on vacation together</u> every summer.

    a. Ted and Janice, who had been friends for years, went on vacation together every summer.

    b. Ted and Janice who had been friends for years, went on vacation together every summer.

    c. Ted, and Janice who had been friends for years, went on vacation together every summer.

    d. None of the choices are correct.

2. None of us want to go to the <u>party not even</u> if there will be live music.

    a. None of us want to go to the party not even, if there will be live music.

    b. None of us want to go to the party, not even if there will be live music.

    c. None of us want to go to the party; not even if there will be live music.

    d. None of the choice are correct.

3. <u>John, Maurice, and Thomas,</u> quit school two months before graduation.

    a. John, Maurice, and Thomas quit school two months before graduation.

    b. John, Maurice and Thomas quit school two months before graduation.

    c. John Maurice and Thomas, quit school two months before graduation.

    d. None of the choice are correct.

4. **"My father said that he would be there on <u>Sunday,"</u> <u>Lee</u> explained.**

    a. "My father said that he would be there on Sunday" Lee explained.

    b. None of the choices are correct.

    c. "My father said that he would be there on Sunday," Lee explained.

    d. "My father said that he would be there on Sunday." Lee explained.

5. **I own two <u>dogs, a cat, named Jeffrey and Henry, the goldfish.</u>**

    a. I own two dogs, a cat named Jeffrey, and Henry, the goldfish.

    b. I own two dogs a cat, named Jeffrey, and Henry, the goldfish.

    c. I own two dogs, a cat named Jeffrey; and Henry, the goldfish.

    d. None of the choices are correct.

6. **Choose the sentence below with the correct punctuation.**

    a. Marcus who won the debate tournament, is the best speaker that I know.

    b. Marcus, who won the debate tournament, is the best speaker that I know.

    c. Marcus who won the debate tournament is the best speaker that I know.

    d. Marcus who won the debate tournament is the best speaker, that I know.

Part II - Sentence Structure and Grammar

Combine the sentences below into one sentence with the same meaning.

7. I hate needles. I want to give blood. I can't give blood.

   a. Although I hate needles, I couldn't give blood even if I wanted to.

   b. Because I hate needles, I can't give blood, although I want to give blood.

   c. Whenever I hate needles, I give blood although I can't give blood.

   d. Whenever I can't give blood, I give blood anyway, although I hate needles.

8. The doctor was not looking forward to meeting Mrs. Lucas. The doctor would have to tell Mrs. Lucas that she has cancer. The doctor hates giving bad news to patients.

   a. The doctor hates giving bad news, so he was not looking forward to meeting Mrs. Lucas and telling her she has cancer.

   b. The doctor has cancer and was not looking forward to meeting Mrs. Lucas and telling her the bad news.

   c. Before the doctor met Mrs. Lucas, he had to give his the patients the bad news that Mrs. Lucas has cancer.

   d. The doctor was not looking forward to giving the bad news to his patients that he had to tell Mrs. Lucas that his patients have cancer.

9. Mom hates shopping. We were out of bread, milk and eggs. Mom went to the supermarket.

    a. Because we were out of bread, milk and eggs, Mom hated shopping at the supermarket.

    b. Although she hates shopping, Mom went to the supermarket since we were out of bread, milk and eggs.

    c. Although we were out of bread, milk and eggs, Mom still hated shopping at the supermarket and went there anyway.

    d. Because Mom hated shopping at the supermarket, she went to there to buy her bread, milk and eggs.

10. The ceremony had an emotional <u>affect</u> on the groom, but the bride was not <u>affected</u>.

    a. The ceremony had an emotional effect on the groom, but the bride was not affected.

    b. The ceremony had an emotional affect on the groom, but the bride was not affected.

    c. The ceremony had an emotional effect on the groom, but the bride was not effected.

11. Anna was taller <u>than Luis, but then</u> he grew four inches in three months.

    a. None of the choices are correct.

    b. Anna was taller then Luis, but than he grew four inches in three months.

    c. Anna was taller than Luis, but than he grew four inches, in three months.

    d. Anna was taller than Luis, but then he grew four inches in three months.

12. <u>There</u> second home is in Boca Raton, but <u>they're</u> not <u>there</u> for most of the year.

    a. Their second home is in Boca Raton, but there not their for most of the year.

    b. They're second home is in Boca Raton, but they're not there for most of the year.

    c. Their second home is in Boca Raton, but they're not there for most of the year.

    d. None of the choices are correct.

13. <u>Their</u> going to graduate in June; after that, <u>their</u> best option will be to go <u>there</u>.

    a. They're going to graduate in June; after that, their best option will be to go there.

    b. There going to graduate in June; after that, their best option will be to go there.

    c. They're going to graduate in June; after that, there best option will be to go their.

    d. None of the choices are correct.

14. Your mistaken; that is not you're book.

    a. You're mistaken; that is not you're book.

    b. Your mistaken; that is not your book.

    c. You're mistaken; that is not your book.

    d. None of the choices are correct.

15. You're classes are on the west side of campus, but you're living on the east side.

   a. You're classes are on the west side of campus, but you're living on the east side.

   b. Your classes are on the west side of campus, but your living on the east side.

   c. Your classes are on the west side of campus, but you're living on the east side.

   d. None of the choices are correct.

16. The Chinese lives in one of the world's most populous nations, while a citizen of Bermuda lives in one of the least populous.

   a. The Chinese live in one of the world's most populous nations, while a citizen of Bermuda lives in one of the least populous.

   b. The Chinese lives in one of the world's most populous nations, while a citizen of Bermuda live in one of the least populous.

   c. The Chinese live in one of the world's most populous nations, while a citizen of Bermuda live in one of the least populous.

   d. None of the choices are correct.

17. You shouldn't sit in that chair wearing black pants; I sit the white cat there just a moment ago.

   a. You shouldn't sit in that chair wearing black pants; I set the white cat there just a moment ago.

   b. You shouldn't set in that chair wearing black pants; I sit the white cat there just a moment ago.

   c. You shouldn't set in that chair wearing black pants; I set the white cat there just a moment ago.

   d. None of the choices are correct.

18. We saw the <u>golden gate Bridge in San Francisco.</u>

   a. Golden Gate Bridge in San Francisco
   b. golden gate bridge in San Francisco
   c. Golden gate bridge in San Francisco
   d. None of the choice are correct.

Part III - Sentence Completion and Correction

19. Collecting stamps, _____ and listening to shortwave radio were Rick's main hobbies.

   a. building models
   b. to build models
   c. having built models
   d. build models

20. Every morning, _____, and before the sun comes up, my mother makes herself a cup of cocoa.

   a. after the kids left for school
   b. after the kids leave for school
   c. after the kids have left for school
   d. after the kids will leave for school

21. Elaine promised to bring the camera _____ at the mall yesterday.

   a. by me
   b. with me
   c. at me
   d. to me

Language Arts

22. Following the tornado, telephone poles _____ all over the street.

    a. laid
    b. lied
    c. were lying
    d. were laying

Part IV - Grammar – Sentence Correction

23. She is the <u>most cleverest</u> girl in the class.

    a. She is the most clever girl in the class.
    b. She is the cleverest girl in the class.
    c. She is the most cleverer girl in the class.
    d. None of the above.

24. He <u>lived</u> in California since 1995.

    a. He had lived in California since 1995.
    b. He has been living in California since 1995.
    c. He has living in California since 1995.
    d. None of the above.

25. Please excuse <u>me being</u> late.

    a. Please excuse me for late.
    b. Please excuse my being late.
    c. Please excuse my being lateness.
    d. None of the above.

ANSWER KEY

1. A
Use a comma to separate phrases.

2. B
Use a comma separates independent clauses. None of us wants to go to the party, not even if there will be live music.

3. B
Don't use a comma before 'and' in a list.

4. C
Commas always go with a quote and the use of said, explained etc.

5. A
This is an example if a comma which appears before 'and,' but is disambiguating. Without the comma, the sentence would be "I own two dogs, a cat named Jeffrey and Henry, the goldfish." This means there is a cat named Jeffrey and Henry, and a goldfish with no name mentioned. The comma appears to show the distinction.

I own two dogs, a cat named Jeffrey, and Henry, the goldfish.

6. B
Comma separate phrases.

7. A
These three sentences can be combined using 'although,' and 'even if.'

8. A
These two sentences can be combined into one sentence with two clauses separated by a comma.

9. B
These three sentences can be combined using 'although,' and 'since.'

English Usage

10. A
Affect vs. Effect - Affect is a verb (action) and effect is a noun (thing).

11. D
Than vs. Then – Than is used for comparison, as in, taller than, and then is used for time, as in, but then...

12. C
There vs. their vs. they're. There indicates existence as in, "there are." Their is to indicate possession, as in, "their book." They're is the contraction form of "they are."

13. A
There vs. their vs. they're. There indicates existence as in, "there are." Their is to indicate possession, as in, "their book." They're is the contraction form of "they are."

14. C
Your vs. you're. Your is the possessive form of you. You're is the contraction form of you are.

15. C
Your vs. you're. Your is the possessive form of you. You're is the contraction form of you are.

16. A
Singular subjects. "The Chinese" is plural, and "a citizen of Bermuda" is singular.

17. A
Sit vs. Set. Set requires an object – something to set down. Sit is something that you do, like sit on the chair.

18. A
Always capitalize proper nouns.

Grammar

19. A
Present progressive "building models" is correct in this sentence.

20. C
Past Perfect tense describes a completed action in the past, before another action in the past.

21. D
The preposition 'to' in this sentence means give.

22. C
"Lie" means to recline, and does not take an object. 'Lay' means to place and does take an object. Peter lay the books on the table, or the telephone poles were lying on the road.

23. B
Cleverest is the proper form to express 'most clever.'

24. B
Past perfect continuous, has been living, is proper because the time element, since 1995, and he is still living there now.

25. B
The correct form is, "please excuse me for being late," or, "please excuse my being late."

English Grammar and Punctuation Tutorials

Capitalization

Although many of the rules for capitalization are pretty straight forward, there are several tricky points that are important to review.

Starting a Sentence

Everyone knows that you need to capitalize the first letter of the first word in a sentence, but is it really all that easy to figure out where one sentence starts and another stops? Take these three examples:

That was the moment it really sunk in: There would be no hockey this year.

It was April and that could mean only one thing: baseball.

We played for hours before heading home; everyone felt tired and happy.

In the first example, the first letter after the colon is capitalized while in the second example, it is not. That is because everything after the first example's colon is a complete sentence, while example two's colon there is only one word. In example three you have what could be a complete sentence ("everyone felt tired and happy"), but which is not because it follows a semicolon, making it just another clause instead.

Within a sentence you can have an additional complete sentence if the sentence follows a colon. However, if what could be a complete sentence follows a semicolon, it is a clause and does not get capitalized.

Remember that the same rules apply for quotation marks that apply for colons: A complete sentence inside quotation marks is capitalized, but a single word or phrase is not.

Proper Nouns

The first letter of all proper nouns needs to be capitalized. There are many categories of proper noun. The most common proper nouns are the specific names of people (such as Bill), places (such as Germany) or things (such as Honda Civic). However, there are several less obvious categories of words that should be capitalized as proper nouns.

Historical events such as World War II or the California Gold Rush need to be capitalized.

The names of celestial bodies such as Orion's Belt need to be capitalized.

The names of ethnicities such as African-American or Hispanic need to be capitalized.

Relationship words that replace a person's name such as Mom, Doctor and Mister need to be capitalized. However, this only happens when you use the word to replace the person's name. In the sentence, "My mom went to the store," you do not capitalize it, while in the sentence, "Hey Mom, did you get toothpaste at the store?" you do capitalize it.

Geographical locations are capitalized. This can be tricky because capitalized geographical locations and non-capitalized directions are easy to confuse. Saying, "We drove south for hours," is a direction, so the word "south" should not be capitalized. However, when saying, "While in the United States, we drove to the South to look at Civil War battle fields," you do capitalize the word "South." The difference is that in the first sentence "south" is just the direction you drove. In the second sentence "the South" is a specific region of the United States that formed itself into the Confederacy during the US Civil War.

Proper Adjectives

Proper adjectives are the adjective forms of proper nouns. People from Germany are German; people from Canada are Canadian. German and Canadian are proper adjectives because they are forms of proper nouns that are used to describe other nouns.

Titles of Works

Titles of works are generally capitalized following a specific pattern. Capitalize all the important words in a sentence. Do not capitalize unimportant words such as prepositions and articles.

For example: Alien Spaceship Spotted over Many of the World's Capitals

Notice that the prepositions "over" and "of," and the article "the" are the only non-capitalized words in the sentence.

Punctuation - Colons, Semicolons, Hyphens, Dashes, Parentheses and Apostrophes

Within a sentence there are several different types of punctuation marks that can denote a pause. Each of these punctuation marks has different rules when it comes to its structure and usage, so we will look at each one in turn.

Colons

The colon is used primarily to introduce information. It can start lists such as in the sentence, "There were several things Susan had to get at the store: bread, cereal, lettuce and tomatoes." Or a colon points out specific information, such as in the sentence, "It was only then that the group fully realized what had happened: The Martian invasion had begun."

Note that if the information after the colon is a complete sentence, you capitalize and punctuate it exactly like you would a sentence. If, however, it does not constitute a complete sentence, you don't have to capitalize anything. ("Peering out the window Meredith saw them: zombies.")

SEMICOLONS

Semicolons are super commas. They denote a stronger stop than a comma does, but they are still weaker than a period, not capable of ending a sentence. Semicolons are primarily used to separate independent clauses that are not being separated by a coordinating conjunction. ("Chris went to the store; he bought chips and salsa.") Semicolons can only do this, however, when the ideas in each clause are related. For instance, the sentence, "It's raining outside; my sister went to the movies," is not a proper usage of the semicolon since those clauses have nothing to do with each other.

Semicolons can also be used in lists if one or more element in the list is itself made up of a smaller list. If you want to write a list of things you plan to bring to a picnic, and those things only include a Frisbee, a chair and some pasta salad, you would not need to use a semicolon. However, if you also wanted to bring plastic knives, forks and spoons, you would need to write your sentence like this: "For our picnic I am bringing a Frisbee; a chair; plastic knives, forks and spoons; and some pasta salad."

Using semicolons like this preserves the smaller list that you have in your larger list.

HYPHENS

To join words together to show that they are linked you use hyphens. The most common use of hyphens is to link together words to show that they are working together in a sentence. ("The well-known actor was eating at the table behind us.") This shows explicitly that you are using "well-known" as a single concept and not as two descriptive words in a list.

Hyphens can also be used to split a word in half if you run out of space writing on one line of a page. This is often seen in newspapers and magazines when text is justified to both sides of a page or a column. For example:

> The massive earthquake caused surpris-
>
> ingly little damage in the affected areas.

However, you can only use a hyphen in this way if you split the word between syllables. Often students think that they can use hyphens to break up words wherever they want; this is wrong. For the word "surprisingly" you could have a hyphen between "sur" and "prisingly," "surpris" and "ingly, and between "surprising" and "ly," but nowhere else.

Finally, hyphens can be used to add prefixes to words. This happens a lot in news reports with phrases such as "pro-government troops."

Dashes and Parentheses

Both dashes and parentheses are used to set aside information into parenthetical statements; statements that can be treated as an aside. They do not need to be there for the sentence to make sense, but the information they provide is interesting enough that you feel it should be included. Parentheses are considered stronger than dashes are. (Commas can also be used to separate nonessential information from a sentence, but they are considered to be the weakest of the three.)

As the previous sentence shows, parentheses can surround entire sentences, separating them from the paragraph. Dashes, on the other hand, can separate off the last statement in a sentence. ("Calvin came home and greeted his family for the first time in days—everyone smiled.") Obviously, that last sentence could also be written using a semicolon or as two sentences. The difference is in how you want it to sound to the reader. Should these thoughts be treated as two distinct pieces? Or should everyone smiling at Calvin be part of the main sentence, just separated a bit more strongly—with a slightly longer pause—than a comma could manage?

APOSTROPHES

There are two primary uses of the apostrophe in English: forming contractions and forming possessive nouns.

Contractions are formed by taking two words and combining them together with an apostrophe replacing the missing letters (do not becomes don't), or by shortening an existing word (cannot becomes can't). Apostrophes can

also make contractions by attaching verbs to nouns or pronouns. ("He's going to the store.")

When making singular nouns possessive the general rule is that you add an 's to the end of singular nouns. (This is Tim's bagel.) When dealing with plural nouns that do not end with the letter –s (such as children), the rule is that you also add an 's to the end of the word. (It was the children's favorite movie.) And when dealing with plural nouns that end with the letter –s, you simply add an apostrophe. (My sisters' favorite game is tag.)

However, and this is an important "however" given the controversy it can cause, when dealing with singular words that end with the letter –s (such as circus), there are two standards for how to make them possessive—each with its own grammar books to back it up.

One standard says that you still add an 's to the end of the word. (This is the circus's biggest tent.) The other says that, since the word ends with an –s, it can only get an apostrophe. (This is the circus' biggest tent.) Some style books, such as the Chicago Manual of Style will go so far as to say that the former option is correct, but to avoid inflaming people's passions on the subject, using the latter is perfectly acceptable. The best thing to do is to find out which style the teacher or editor you are writing for at any given time prefers and conform to it for that person.

COMMAS

Commas are probably the most commonly used punctuation mark in English. Commas can break the flow of writing to give it a more natural sounding style, and they are the main punctuation mark used to separate ideas. Commas also separate lists, introductory adverbs, introductory prepositional phrases, dates and addresses.

The most rigid way that commas are used is when separating clauses. There are two primary types of clauses in a sentence, independent and subordinate (sometimes called dependent). Independent clauses are clauses that express a complete thought, such as, "Tim went to the store." Subordinate clauses, on the other hand, only express partial thoughts that expand on an independent clause, such as, "after the game ended," which you can see is clearly not a complete sentence. (You will learn more about clauses in different lessons.)

The rule for commas with clauses is that a comma must separate the clauses when a subordinate clause comes first in a sentence: "After the game ended, Tim went to the store." But there should not be a comma when a subordinate clause follows an independent clause: "Tim went to the store after the game ended." If you leave the comma out of the first example, you have a run-on sentence. If you add one into the second example, you have a comma-splice error. Also, when you have two independent clauses joined with a coordinating conjunction, you need to separate them with a comma. "Tim went to the store, and Beth went home."

There are some artistic exceptions to these rules, such as adding a pause for literary effect, but for the most part, they are set in stone.

Commas are also used to separate items in a list. This area of English is unfortunately less clear than it should be, with two separate rules depending on what standard you are following. To understand the two different rules, let's pretend you are having a party at your house, and you are making a list of refreshments your friends will want. You may decide to serve three things: 1) pizza 2) chips 3) drinks. There are two different rules governing how you should punctuate this. According to many grammar books, you would write this as, "At the store I will buy pizza, chips, and drinks." This variation puts a comma after each item in the list. It is the version that the style books used in most college English and history courses will prefer, so it is probably the one you should follow. However, the Associated Press style guide, which is used in college journalism classes and at newspapers and magazines, says the sentence should be written like this: "At the store I will buy pizza, chips and drinks." Here you only use a comma between the first two words, letting the word "and" act as the separator between the last two.

Another important place to use commas is when you have a modifier that describes an element of a sentence, but that does not directly follow the thing it describes. Look at the sentence: "Tim went over to visit Beth, watching the full moon along the way." In this sentence there is no confusion about who is "watching the full moon"; it is Tim, probably as he walks to Beth's house. If you remove the comma, however, you get this: "Tim went over to visit Beth watching the full moon along the way." Now it sounds as though Beth is watching the full moon, and we are forced to wonder what "way" the moon is traveling along.

Commas are also used when adding introductory prepositional phrases and introductory adverbs to sentences. A comma is always needed following an introductory adverb. ("Quickly, Jody ran to the car.") Commas are even necessary when you have an adverb introducing a clause within a sentence, even if the clause not the first clause of the sentence. ("Amanda wanted to go to the movie; however, she knew her homework was more important.")

With introductory prepositional phrases you only add a comma if the phrase (or if a group of introductory phrases) is five or more words long. Thus, the sentence you just read did not have a comma following its introductory prepositional phrase ("With introductory prepositional phrases") because it was only four words. Compare that to this sentence with a five word introductory phrase: "After the ridiculously long class, the friends needed to relax."

The last main way that commas are used in sentences is to separate out information that does not need to be there. For instance, "My cousin Hector, who wore a blue hat at the party, thought you were funny." The fact that Hector wore a blue hat is interesting, but it is not vital to the sentence; it could be removed and not changed the sentence's meaning. Therefore it gets commas around it. Along these lines you should remember that any clause introduced by the word that is considered to provide essential information to the sentence and should not get commas around it. Conversely, any clause starting with the word which is considered non-essential and should not get commas around it.

Quotation Marks

Quotation marks are used in English in a variety of different ways. The most common use of quotation marks is to show quotations either as dialogue or when directly quoting a source in an essay or news article. Fortunately, both of these uses follow the same basic rules.

When you have a quote written as the second part of a sentence, you need to put a comma before the quotation marks and a period inside the quotation marks at the end. (Franklin said, "Let's go to the store.") Conversely, when you have quote as the first part of the sentence with information describing it second, a comma replaces the period at the end of the sentence inside the quotes. ("Let's go to the store," Franklin said.)

If the information in a quote is not a complete sentence, you do not need to capitalize it or put commas around it, if it is not dialogue. (No one thought the idea of "going to the store" sounded very fun.)

Note that when the last word in a sentence has both a quotation mark and a period attached to it, the period is always inside the quotes. This is the case when you have a complete sentence inside a quote ("Let's go to the store."), and when the last word in a sentence just happens to have quote marks around it (Kerri said I was "mean.") You also need to do the same thing with commas. (Kerri said I was "mean," and it made me feel bad.) However, other punctuation marks such as colons, semicolons and dashes do not follow this rule and should come outside the quotes. (Kerri said I was "mean"; it made me feel bad.)

When you want to use a quote inside a quote, you use the standard double-quotation marks for the outer quote and single-quotation marks for the inner quote. ("The sign on the door said 'no soliciting,' so we went to the next house.")

Quotation marks are also used around certain types of titles. To figure out which ones, it helps to look at which titles are not put in quotes as well.

Titles have two categories: large works and small works. Large works are things such as newspapers, magazines, CDs, books and television shows. The defining characteristic of a large work is that it is able to hold small works in it. Small works are the articles inside newspapers and magazines, the songs on a CD, the chapters in a book and the episodes of a television show. It is small works that get quotation marks around them. (Large works, meanwhile, are either underlined or italicized.)

Using quotation marks correctly in a title looks something like this: The two-page article entitled "San Francisco Giants Win World Series" appeared in yesterday's New York Times. The article title is in quotes, and the newspaper title is in italics.

How to Answer English Grammar Multiple Choice - Verb Tense

This tutorial is designed to help you answer English Grammar multiple choice questions as well as a very quick refresher on verb tenses. It is assumed that you have some familiarity with the verb tenses covered here. If you find these questions difficulty or do not understand the tense construction, we recommend you seek out additional instruction.

Tenses Covered

1. Past Progressive
2. Present Perfect
3. Present Perfect Progressive
4. Present Progressive
5. Simple Future
6. Simple Future – "Going to" Form
7. Past Perfect Progressive
8. Future Perfect Progressive
9. Future Perfect
10. Future Progressive
11. Past Perfect

1. The Past Progressive Tense

How to Recognize This Tense

He *was running* very fast when he fell.

They *were drinking* coffee when he arrived.

About the Past Progressive Tense

This tense is used to speak of an action that was in progress in the past when another event occurred.

The action was unfolding at a point in the past.

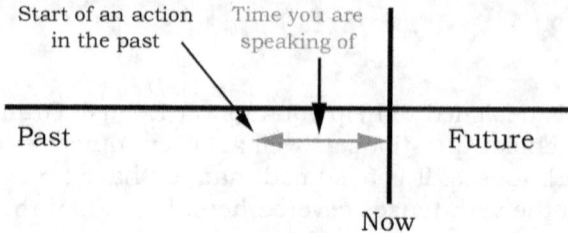

Past Progressive Tense Construction

This tense is formed by using the past tense of the verb "to be" plus the present participle of the main verb.

Sample Question

Bill _____ lunch when we arrived.

    a. will eat

    b. is eating

    c. eats

    d. was eating

How to Answer This Type of Question

1. First examine the question for clues about the time frame.

The sentence ends with "when we arrived," so we know the time frame is a point ("when") in the past (arrived).

The correct answer will refer to an ongoing action at a point of time in the past.

2. Examine the choices and eliminate any obviously incorrect answers.

Choice A is the future tense so we can eliminate.

Choice B is the present continuous so we can eliminate.

Choice C is present tense so we can eliminate.

Choice D refers to an action that takes place at a point of time in the past ("was eating").

2. THE PRESENT PERFECT TENSE

How to Recognize This Tense

I *have had* enough to eat.

We *have been* to Paris many times.

I *have known* him for five years.

I *have been* coming here since I was a child.

About the Present Perfect Tense

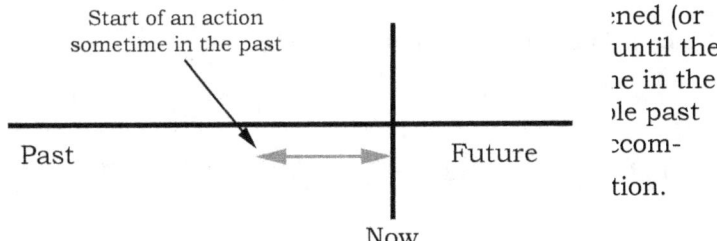

Present Perfect Tense Construction

It is also used with "for" and "since."

This tense is formed by using the present tense of the verb

"to have" plus the past participle of the main verb.

Sample Question

I _____ these birds many times.

    a. am seeing

    b. will saw

    c. have seen

    d. have saw

How to Answer This Type of Question

1. First examine the question for clues about the time frame.

"Many times" tells us that the action is repeated and in the past.

2. Examine the choices and eliminate any obviously incorrect answers.

Choice A, "am seeing" is incorrect because it is a continuing action, i.e. in the present; it also doesn't use a form of 'have'.

Choice B is grammatically incorrect.

Choice C tells of something that has happened in the past and is now over. Best choice so far.

Choice D is grammatically incorrect.

3. THE PRESENT PERFECT PROGRESSIVE TENSE

How to Recognize This Tense

We *have been seeing* a lot of rainy days.

I *have been reading* some very good books.

About the Present Perfect Progressive Tense

This tense expresses the idea that something happened (or action is happening) in the past and continues into the present. The action started sometime in the past and continues up to now.

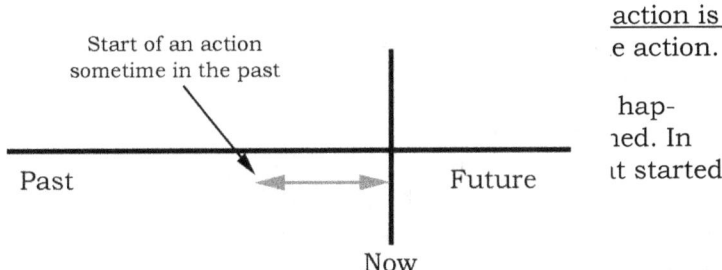

Present Perfect Progressive Tense Construction

This tense is formed by using the present tense of the verb "to have," plus "been," plus the present participle of the main verb.

Sample Question

Bill _____ there for two hours.

    a. sits

    b. sitting

    c. has been sitting

    d. will sat

How to Answer This Type of Question

1. First examine the question for clues about the time frame.

"For two hours" tells us that the action, "sits," is continuous up to now, and may continue into the future.

Note this sentence could also be the simple past tense,

Bill sat there for two hours.

Or the future tense,

Bill will sit there for two hours.

However, these are not among the choices.

2. Examine the choices and eliminate any obviously incorrect answers.

Choice A is incorrect because it is the present tense.
Choice B is incorrect because it is the present continuous.
Choice C is correct. "Has been sitting" expresses a continuous action in the past that isn't finished.
Choice D is grammatically incorrect.

4. THE PRESENT PROGRESSIVE TENSE

How to Recognize This Tense

We *are having* a delicious lunch.

They *are driving* much too fast.

About the Present Progressive Tense

This tense is used to express what the action is <u>right now</u>. The action started in the recent past, and is continuing into the future.

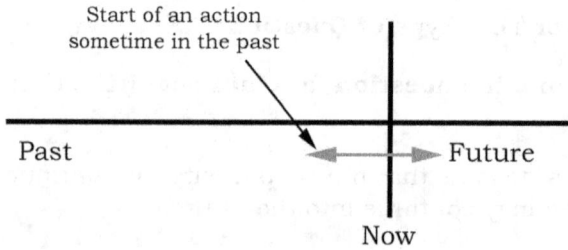

Present Perfect Tense Construction

The Present Progressive Tense is formed by using the present tense of "to be" plus the present participle of the main verb.

Sample Question

She _____ very hard these days.

    a. works

    b. is working

    c. will work

    d. worked

How to Answer This Type of Question

1. First examine the question for clues about the time frame.

The end of the sentence includes "these days" which tell us the action started in the past, continues into the present, and may continue into the future.

2. Examine the choices and eliminate any obviously incorrect answers.

Choice A, the simple present is incorrect.
Choice B, "is working" is correct.
Check the other two choices just to be sure. Choice C is future tense, and Choice D is past tense, so they can be eliminated.

The correct answer is Choice B.

5. THE SIMPLE FUTURE TENSE

How to Recognize This Tense

I *will see* you tomorrow.
We *will drive* the car.

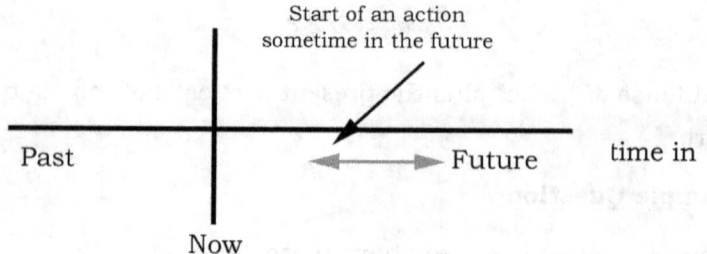

Simple Future Tense Construction

The tense is formed by using "will" plus the root form of the verb. (The root form of the verb is the infinitive without "to." Examples: read, swim.)

Sample Question

We _____ to Paris next year.

    a. went

    b. had been

    c. will go

    d. go

How to Answer This Type of Question

1. First examine the question for clues about the time frame.

The last two words of the sentence, "next year," clearly identify this sentence as referring to the future.

2. Examine the choices and eliminate any obviously incorrect answers.

Choice A is the past tense and can be eliminated.

Choice B is the past perfect tense and can be eliminated.

Choice D is the simple present and can be eliminated.

Choice C is the only one left and is the correct simple future tense.

6. The Simple Future Tense – The "Going to" Form

How to Recognize This Tense

I *am going to* see you tomorrow.

We *are going to* drive the car.

About the Simple Future Tense

This form of the future tense is used to show the intention of doing something in the future. (This is the strict grammatical meaning, but in daily speech, it is often used interchangeably with the simple future tense, the "will" form.)

The tense is formed by using the present conditional tense of "to go," plus the infinitive of the verb.

Sample Question

I _____ shopping in an hour.

    a. go

    b. have gone

    c. am going to go

    d. went

How to Answer This Type of Question

1. First examine the question for clues about the time frame.

"In an hour" clearly identifies the action as taking place in the future.

2. Examine the choices and eliminate any obviously incorrect answers.

Choice A is the simple present tense and can be eliminated.

Choice B is the past perfect and can be eliminated.

Choice C is the correct answer.

Choice D is the past tense and can be eliminated.

7. THE PAST PERFECT PROGRESSIVE TENSE

How to Recognize This Tense

I *had been sleeping* for an hour when you phoned.

We *had been eating* our dinner when they all came into the

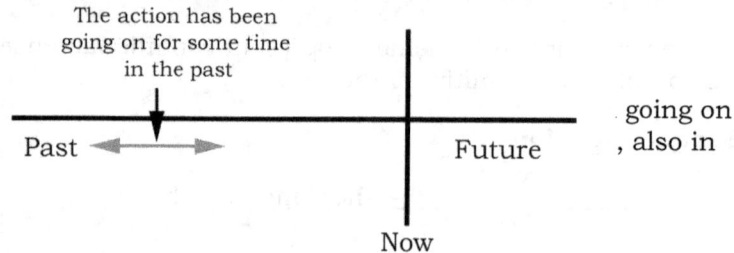

Past Perfect Tense Construction

The tense is formed by using the past perfect tense of the verb "to be" plus the present participle of the main verb.

Sample Question

How long _____ you _____ when I saw you?

    a. are _____ running
    b. had _____ running
    c. had _____ been running
    d. was _____ running

How to Answer This Type of Question

1. First examine the question for clues about the time frame.

"When I saw" tells us the sentence happened at a point of time ("when") in the past ("saw").

2. Examine the choices and eliminate any obviously incorrect answers.

Choice A, "are running" is incorrect and can be eliminated.

Choice B, "Had ___ running" is grammatically incorrect and can be eliminated.

Choice C is correct.

Choice D is grammatically incorrect so the answer is Choice C.

8. Future Perfect Progressive Tense

How to Recognize This Tense

I *will have been working* here for two years in March.

I *will have been driving* for four hours when I get there, so I will be tired.

About the Future Perfect Progressive Tense

This tense is used to show that the action continues up to a point of time in the future.

Future Prefect Progressive Tense Construction

This tense is formed by using the future perfect tense of "to be" plus the present participle of the main verb.

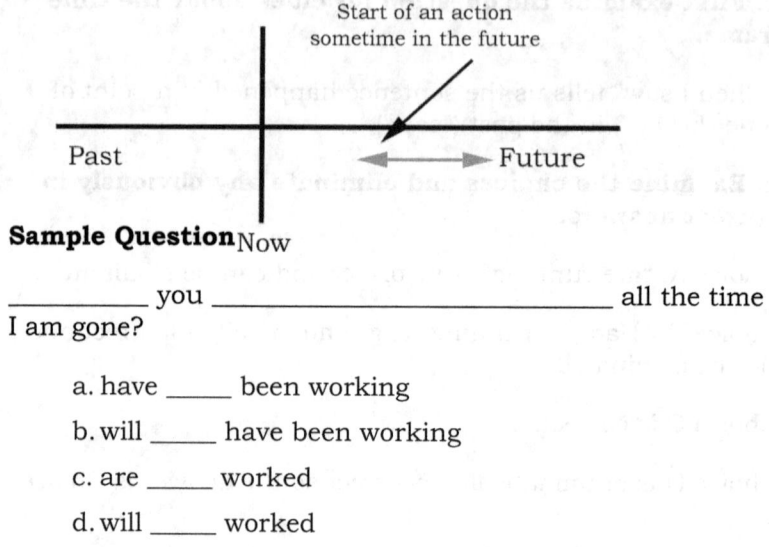

Sample Question

_____ you _____ all the time I am gone?

      a. have _____ been working
      b. will _____ have been working
      c. are _____ worked
      d. will _____ worked

How to Answer This Type of Question

1. First examine the question for clues about the time frame.

"All the time I am gone" refers to an action in the future ("time I am gone") and the action is progressive ("all the time"). The progressive action means the correct choice will be a verb tense that ends in "ing."

2. Examine the choices and eliminate any obviously incorrect answers.

Choice A, the past perfect, refers to a past continuous event and is also grammatically incorrect in the sentence, so Choice A can be eliminated.

Choice B looks correct because it refers to an action will be going on for a period of time in the future.

Examine Choices C and D just to be sure. Both choices are grammatically incorrect and can be eliminated.
Choice B is the correct answer.

9. THE FUTURE PERFECT TENSE

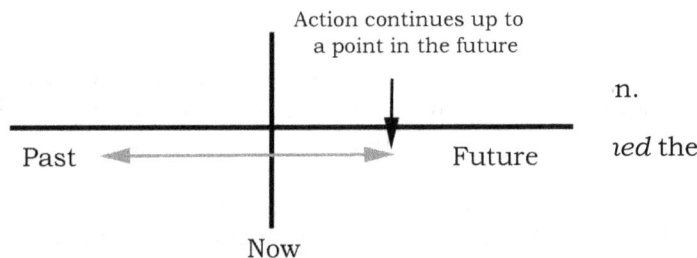

About the Future Perfect Tense

The future perfect tense expresses action in the future before another action in the future. This is the past in the future.

For example:

He *will have prepared* dinner when she arrives.

Future Perfect Tense Construction

This tense is formed by "will + have + past participle."

Sample Question

They _____ their seats before the game begins.

    a. will have find
    b. will find
    c. will have found
    d. found

How to Answer This Type of Question

1. First examine the question for clues about the time frame.

This question could be several different tenses. The only clue about the time frame is "before the game begins," which refers to a specific point of time.

We know it isn't in the past, because "begins" is incorrect for the past tense. Similarly with the present. So the question is about something that happens in the future, before another event in the future.

2. Examine the choices and eliminate any obviously incorrect answers.

Choice A can be eliminated as incorrect.
Choice B looks good, so mark it and check the others before making a final decision.
Choice C is the past perfect and can be eliminated because the time frame is incorrect.
Choice D is the simple past tense and can be eliminated for the same reason.

10. FUTURE PROGRESSIVE TENSE

How to Recognize This Tense

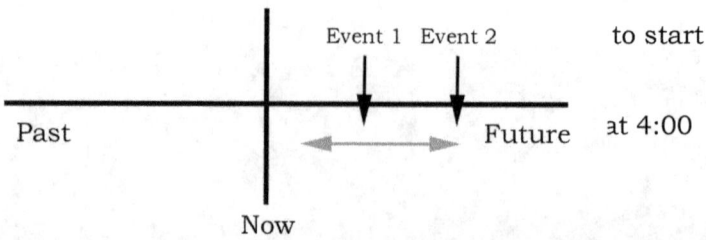

About the Future Progressive Tense

The future progressive tense talks about a continuing action in the future.

Future Progressive Tense Construction

will+ be + (root form) + ing = will be playing

Sample Question

Many excited fans _____ a bus to see the game at 4:00.

    a. catch

    b. catching

    c. have been catching

    d. will be catching

How to Answer This Type of Question

1. First examine the question for clues about the time frame.

"At 4:00," tells us the sentence is either in the past OR in the future.

2. Examine the choices and eliminate any obviously incorrect answers.

From the time frame of the sentence, the answer will be past or future tense.
Choice A is the present tense and can be eliminated.
Choice B is the present continuous tense and can be eliminated.
Choice C is the past perfect continuous and can be eliminated.
Choice D is the only one left. Quickly examining the tense, it is future progressive and is correct in the sentence.

11. THE PAST PERFECT TENSE

How to Recognize This Tense

The party *had* just *started* when the coach arrived.

We *had waited* for twenty minutes when the bus finally came.

About the Past Perfect

The past perfect tense talks about two events that happened   irst.

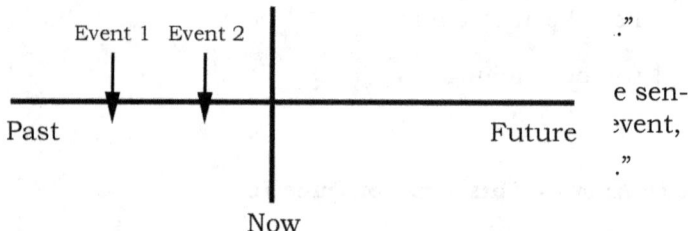

I had already eaten when my friends arrived.

Past Perfect Tense Construction

The past perfect is formed by "have" plus the past participle.

Sample Question

It was time to go home after they _____ the game.

    a. will win
    b. win
    c. had won
    d. wins

How to Answer This Type of Question

1. First examine the question for clues about the time frame.

"Was" tells us the sentence happened in the past. Also notice there are two events, "go home" and "after the game."

2. Examine the choices and eliminate any obviously incorrect answers.

Choice A is the future tense and can be eliminated. Choice B is the simple present and can be eliminated. Choice C is the past perfect and orders the two events in the past. Choice D is the present tense and incorrect and can be eliminated, so Choice C is the correct answer.

COMMON ENGLISH USAGE MISTAKES - A QUICK REVIEW

Like some parts of English grammar, usage is definitely going to be on the exam and there isn't any tricky strategies or shortcuts to help you get through this section.

Here is a quick review of common usage mistakes.

1. MAY AND MIGHT

'May' can act as a principal verb, which can express permission or possibility.

Examples:

Lets wait, the meeting may have started.
May I begin now?

'May' can act as an auxiliary verb, which expresses a purpose or wish.

Examples:

May you find favour in the sight of your employer.

May your wishes come true.
People go to school so that they may be educated.

The past tense of may is might.

Examples:

I asked if I might begin

'Might' can be used to signify a weak or slim possibility or polite suggestion.

Examples:

You might find him in his office, but I doubt it.
You might offer to help if you want to.

2. LIE AND LAY

The verb lay should always take an object. The three forms of the verb lay are: laid, lay and laid.

The verb lie (recline) should not take any object. The three forms of the verb lie are: lay, lie and lain.

Examples:

Lay on the bed.
The tables were laid by the students.
Let the little kid lie.
The patient lay on the table.

The dog has lain there for 30 minutes.

Note: The verb lie can also mean "to tell a falsehood." This verb can appear in three forms: lied, lie, and lied. This is different from the verb lie (recline) mentioned above.

Examples:

The accused is fond of telling lies.
Did she lie?

3. WOULD AND SHOULD

The past tense of shall is 'should', and so "should" generally follows the same principles as "shall."

The past tense of will is "would," and so "would" generally follows the same principles as "will."

The two verbs 'would and should' can be correctly used interchangeably to signify obligation. The two verbs also have some unique uses too. Should is used in three persons to signify obligation.

Examples:

I should go after work.
People should exercise everyday.
You should be generous.

"Would" is specially used in any of the three persons, to signify willingness, determination and habitual action.

Examples:

They would go for a test run every Saturday.
They would not ignore their duties.

She would try to be punctual.

4. Principle and Auxiliary Verbs

Two principal verbs can be used along with one auxiliary verb as long as the auxiliary verb form suits the two principal verbs.

Examples:

Several people have been employed and some promoted.

A new tree has been planted and the old has been cut down.

Again note the difference in the verb form.

5. Can and Could

A. Can is used to express capacity or ability.

Examples:

I can complete the assignment today
He can meet his target.

B. Can is also used to express permission.

Examples:

Yes, you can begin

In the sentence below, "can" was used to mean the same thing as "may." However, the difference is that the word "can" is used for negative or interrogative sentences, while "may" is used in affirmative sentences to express possibility.

Examples:

They may be correct.   Positive sentence - use may.
Can this statement be correct? A question using "can."
It cannot be correct. Negative sentence using "can."

The past tense of can is could. It can serve as a principal verb when it is used to express its own meaning.

Examples:

Despite the difficulty of the test, he could still perform well. "Could" here is used to express ability.

6. OUGHT

The verb ought should normally be followed by the word to.

Examples:

I *ought to* close shop now.

The verb 'ought' expresses:
A. Desirability

You ought to wash your hands before eating.   It is desirable to wash your hands.

B. Probability

She ought to be on her way back by now.   She is probably on her way.

C. Moral obligation or duty

The government ought to protect the oppressed.   It is the government's duty to protect the oppressed.

7. RAISE AND RISE

Rise
The verb rise means to go up, or to ascend.
The verb rise can appear in three forms, rose, rise, and risen. The verb should not take an object.

Examples:

The bird rose very slowly.
The trees rise above the house.
My aunt has risen in her career.

Raise
The verb raise means to increase, to lift up.
The verb raise can appear in three forms, raised, raise and raised.

Examples:

He raised his hand.
The workers requested a raise.
Do not raise that subject.

8. PAST TENSE AND PAST PARTICIPLE

Pay attention to the proper use of these verbs: sing, show, ring, awake, fly, flow, begin, hang and sink.

Mistakes usually occur when using the past participle and past tense of these verbs as they are often mixed up.

Each of these verbs can appear in three forms:

Sing, Sang, Sung.

Show, Showed, Showed/Shown.
Ring, Rang, Rung.
Awake, awoke, awaken
Fly, Flew, Flown.
Flow, Flowed, Flowed.
Begin, Began, Begun.
Hang, Hanged, Hanged (a criminal)
Hang, Hung, Hung (a picture)
Sink, Sank, Sunk.

Examples:

The stranger rang the door bell. (simple past tense)
I have rung the door bell already. (past participle - an action completed in the past)

The stone sank in the river. (simple past tense)
The stone had already sunk. (past participle - an action completed in the past)
The meeting began at 4:00.

The meeting has begun.

9. SHALL AND WILL

When speaking informally, the two can be used interchangeably. In formal writing, they must be used correctly.

"Will" is used in the second or third person, while "shall" is used in the first person. Both verbs are used to express a time or even in the future.

Examples:

I shall, We shall (First Person)
You will (Second Person)
They will (Third Person)

This principle however reverses when the verbs are to be used to express threats, determination, command, willingness, promise or compulsion. In these instances, will is now used in first person and shall in the second and third person.

Examples:

I will be there next week, no matter what.
This is a promise, so the first person "I" takes "will."

You shall ensure that the work is completed.
This is a command, so the second person "you" takes "shall."

I will try to make payments as promised.
This is a promise, so the first person "I" takes "will."

They shall have arrived by the end of the day.
This is a determination, so the third person "they" takes shall.

Note
A. The two verbs, shall and will should not occur twice in the same sentence when the same future is being referred to

Example:

I shall arrive early if my driver is here on time.

B. Will should not be used in the first person when questions are being asked

Examples:

Shall I go ?
Shall we go?

Subject Verb Agreement

Verbs in any sentence must agree with the subject of the sentence in person and number. Problems usually occur when the verb doesn't correspond with the right subject or the verb fails to match the noun close to it.

Unfortunately, there is no easy way around these principals - no tricky strategy or easy rule. You just have to memorize them.

Here is a quick review:

The verb to be, present (past)

Person	Singular	Plural
First	I am (was)	we are (were)
Second	you are (were)	you are (were)
Third	he, she, it is (was)	they are (were)

The verb to have, present (past)

Person	Singular	Plural
First	I have (had)	we have (had)
Second	you have (had)	you have (had)
Third	he, she, it has (had)	they have (had)

Regular verbs, e.g. to walk, present (past)

Person	Singular	Plural
First	I walk (walked)	we walk (walked)
Second	you walk (walked)	you walk (walked)
Third	he, she, it walks (walked)	they work (walked)

1. Every and Each

When nouns are qualified by "every" or "each," they take a singular verb even if they are joined by 'and'

Examples:

Each mother and daughter *was* a given separate test.
Every teacher and student *was* properly welcomed.

2. Plural Nouns

Nouns like measles, tongs, trousers, riches, scissors etc. are all plural.

Examples:

The trousers *are* dirty.
My scissors *have* gone missing.
The tongs *are* on the table.

3. With and As Well

Two subjects linked by "with" or "as well" should have a verb that matches the first subject.

Examples:

The pencil, with the papers and equipment, *is* on the desk.
David as well as Louis is coming.

4. Plural Nouns

The following nouns take a singular verb:

politics, mathematics, innings, news, advice, summons, furniture, information, poetry, machinery, vacation, scenery

Examples:

The machinery *is* difficult to assemble
The furniture *has* been delivered
The scenery *was* beautiful

5. Single Entities

A proper noun in plural form that refers to a single entity requires a singular verb. This is a complicated way of saying; some things appear to be plural, but are really singular, or some nouns refer to a collection of things but the collection is really singular.

Examples:

The United Nations Organization *is* the decision maker in the matter.

Here the "United Nations Organization" is really only one "thing" or noun, but is made up of many "nations."

The book, "The Seven Virgins" *was* not available in the library.

Here there is only one book, although the title of the book is plural.

6. SPECIFIC AMOUNTS ARE ALWAYS SINGULAR

A plural noun that refers to a specific amount or quantity that is considered as a whole (dozen, hundred, score etc) requires a singular verb.

Examples:

60 minutes *is* quite a long time.
Here "60 minutes" is considered a whole, and therefore one item (singular noun).
The first million is the most difficult.

7. EITHER, NEITHER AND EACH ARE ALWAYS SINGULAR

The verb is always singular when used with: either, each, neither, every one and many.

Examples:

Either of the boys *is* lying.
Each of the employees *has* been well compensated

Many a police officer *has* been found to be courageous
Every one of the teachers *is* responsible

8. LINKING WITH EITHER, OR, AND NEITHER MATCH THE SECOND SUBJECT

Two subjects linked by "either," "or,""nor" or "neither" should have a verb that matches the second subject.

Examples:

Neither David nor Paul *will* be coming.
Either Mary or Tina *is* paying.

Note
If one subject linked by "either," "or,""nor" or "neither" is in plural form, then the verb should also be in plural, and the verb should be close to the plural subject.

Examples:
Neither the mother *nor* her kids *have* eaten.
Either Mary *or* her *friends are* paying.

9. COLLECTIVE NOUNS ARE PLURAL

Some collective nouns such as poultry, gentry, cattle, vermin etc. are considered plural and require a plural verb.

Examples:

The *poultry are* sick.
The *cattle are* well fed.

Note
Collective nouns involving people can work with both plural and singular verbs.

Examples:

Nigerians are known to be hard working
Europeans live in Africa

10. Nouns that are Singular and Plural

Nouns like deer, sheep, swine, salmon etc. can be singular or plural and require the same verb form.

Examples:

The swine is feeding. (singular)
The swine are feeding. (plural)

The salmon is on the table. (singular)
The salmon are running upstream. (plural)

11. Collective Nouns are Singular

Collective nouns such as Army, Jury, Assembly, Committee, Team etc should carry a singular verb when they subscribe to one idea. If the ideas or views are more than one, then the verb used should be plural.

Examples:

The committee is in agreement in their decision.

The committee were in disagreement in their decision.
The jury has agreed on a verdict.
The jury were unable to agree on a verdict.

12. SUBJECTS LINKS BY "AND" ARE PLURAL.

Two subjects linked by "and" always require a plural verb

Examples:

David and John are students.

Note
If the subjects linked by "and" are used as one phrase, or constitute one idea, then the verb must be singular

The color of his socks and shoe is black.
Here "socks and shoe" are two nouns, however the subject is "color" which is singular.

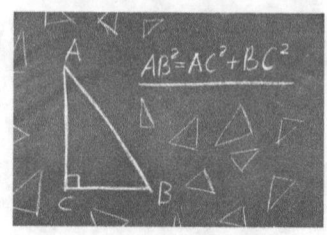

MATHEMATICS

THIS SECTION CONTAINS A SELF-ASSESSMENT AND MATH TUTORIALS. The Tutorials are designed to familiarize general principles and the Self-Assessment contains general questions similar to the math questions likely to be on the CHSPE exam, but are not intended to be identical to the exam questions. The tutorials are not designed to be a complete math course, and it is assumed that students have some familiarity with math. If you do not understand parts of the tutorial, or find the tutorial difficult, it is recommended that you seek out additional instruction.

TOUR OF THE CHSPE MATHEMATICS CONTENT

The CHSPE mathematics section has 50 questions. Below is a detailed list of the mathematics topics likely to appear on the CHSPE. Make sure that you understand these topics at the very minimum.

- Convert decimals, percent, and fractions

- Solve word problems

- Calculate percent and ratio

- Operations using fractions, percent and decimals

- Analyze and interpret tables, graphs and charts

- Data and Statistics

- Geometry and measurement

- Understand and solve simple algebra problems

The questions in the self-assessment are not the same as you will find on the CHSPE - that would be too easy! And nobody knows what the questions will be and they change all the time. Mostly, the changes consist of substituting new questions for old, but the changes also can be new question formats or styles, changes to the number of questions in each section, changes to the time limits for each section, and combining sections. So, while the format and exact wording of the questions may differ slightly, and changes from year to year, if you can answer the questions below, you will have no problem with the mathematics section of the CHSPE.

MATHEMATICS SELF-ASSESSMENT

The purpose of the self-assessment is:

- Identify your strengths and weaknesses.

- Develop your personalized study plan (above)

- Get accustomed to the CHSPE® format

- Extra practice – the self-assessments are almost a full 3rd practice test!

- Provide a baseline score for preparing your study schedule.

Since this is a Self-assessment, and depending on how confident you are with mathematics, timing yourself is optional. The CHSPE has 50 questions, to be answered in 60 minutes. This self-assessment has 30 questions, so allow about 35 minutes to complete.

Once complete, use the table below to assess your understanding of the content, and prepare your study schedule described in chapter 1.

80% - 100%	Excellent – you have mastered the content
60 – 79%	Good. You have a working knowledge. Even though you can just pass this section, you may want to review the Tutorials and do some extra practice to see if you can improve your mark.
40% - 59%	Below Average. You do not understand the content. Review the tutorials, and retake this quiz again in a few days, before proceeding to the rest of the Practice Test Questions.
Less than 40%	Poor. You have a very limited understanding. Please review the Tutorials, and retake this quiz again in a few days, before proceeding to the Practice Test Questions.

MATH SELF-ASSESSMENT

	A	B	C	D	E		A	B	C	D	E
1	○	○	○	○	○	21	○	○	○	○	○
2	○	○	○	○	○	22	○	○	○	○	○
3	○	○	○	○	○	23	○	○	○	○	○
4	○	○	○	○	○	24	○	○	○	○	○
5	○	○	○	○	○	25	○	○	○	○	○
6	○	○	○	○	○						
7	○	○	○	○	○						
8	○	○	○	○	○						
9	○	○	○	○	○						
10	○	○	○	○	○						
11	○	○	○	○	○						
12	○	○	○	○	○						
13	○	○	○	○	○						
14	○	○	○	○	○						
15	○	○	○	○	○						
16	○	○	○	○	○						
17	○	○	○	○	○						
18	○	○	○	○	○						
19	○	○	○	○	○						
20	○	○	○	○	○						

MATH SELF-ASSESSMENT

DECIMALS, FRACTIONS AND PERCENT

1. 15 is what percent of 200?

    a. 7.50%
    b. 15%
    c. 20%
    d. 17.50%

2. A boy has 5 red balls, 3 white balls and 2 yellow balls. What percent of the balls are yellow?

    a. 2%
    b. 8%
    c. 20%
    d. 12%

3. Add 10% of 300 to 50% of 20

    a. 50%
    b. 40%
    c. 60%
    d. 45%

4. Convert 75% to a fraction.

    a. 2/100
    b. 85/100
    c. 3/4
    d. 4/7

5. Convert 90% to a fraction

　　a. 1/10
　　b. 9/9
　　c. 10/100
　　d. 9/10

6. Multiply 3 by 25% of 40

　　a. 75
　　b. 30
　　c. 68
　　d. 35

7. Convert 0.28 to a fraction.

　　a. 7/25
　　b. 3.25
　　c. 8/25
　　d. 5/28

8. Convert 0.45 to a fraction

　　a. 7/20
　　b. 7/45
　　c. 9/20
　　d. 3/20

9. Convert 1/5 to percent.

　　a. 10%
　　b. 5%
　　c. 20%
　　d. 25%

10. Convert 4/20 to percent

a. 25%
b. 20%
c. 40%
d. 30%

11. A man buys an item for $420 and has a balance of 3000.00. How much did he have before?

a. $2,580
b. $3,420
c. $2,420
d. $342

12. Divide 9.60 by 3.2

a. 2.50
b. 3
c. 2.3
d. 6.4

Basic Algebra

13. If X = 7 solve 3x + 5 − 2x

a. x = 6
b. x = 12
c. x = 1
d. x = 0

14. $(x - 2) / 4 - (3x + 5) / 7 = -3$, x=?

    a. 6
    b. 7
    c. 10
    d. 13

15. Expand (x + 7) (x - 3)

    a. $x^2 + 4x - 21$
    b. x + 21
    c. $2x^2 + 4 - 21$
    d. 6x - 21 2x + 4x - 21

16. Find the solution to this inequality x + 3 > 12

    a. x < 9
    b. x > 9
    c. x = 9
    d. x = 10

17. Estimate 5205 / 25

    a. 108
    b. 308
    c. 208
    d. 408

EXPONENTS

18. Express in 3^4 standard form

    a. 81
    b. 27
    c. 12
    d. 9

19. Simplify $4^3 + 2^4$

    a. 45
    b. 108
    c. 80
    d. 48

20. If x = 2 and y = 5, solve $xy^3 - x^3$

    a. 240
    b. 258
    c. 248
    d. 242

21. $X^3 \times X^2$

    a. 5^x
    b. x^{-5}
    c. x^{-1}
    d. X^5

22. Express 100000⁰ standard form

   a. 1
   b. 0
   c. 100000
   d. 1000

PROBABILITY

23. A girl has 4 red, 5 green and 2 yellow balls. She chooses two balls randomly. What is the probability that one is red and other is green?

   a. 2/11
   b. 19/22
   c. 20/121
   d. 9/11

24. In a class of 83 students, 72 are present. What percent of the students are absent? Provide answer up to two significant digits.

   a. 12
   b. 13
   c. 14
   d. 15

25. Britney tossed a coin 10 times and observed 6 heads and 4 tails. What are the chances she will get heads on the next toss?

   a. 1/2
   b. 1/3
   c. 6/10
   d. 4/10

GEOMETRY

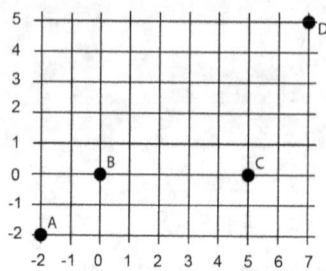

26. Which of the above points represents the origin?

    a. A
    b. B
    c. C
    d. D

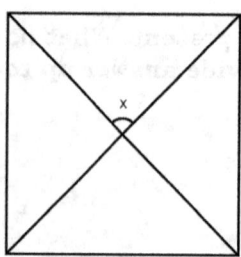

27. What is measurement of the indicated angle?

    a. 45°
    b. 90°
    c. 60°
    d. 30°

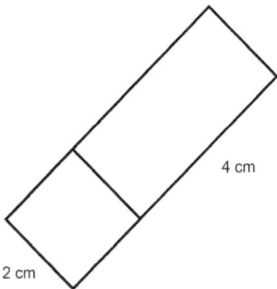

Note: figure not drawn to scale.

28. Assuming the figure with side 2 cm. is square, what is the perimeter of the above shape?

    a. 12 cm
    b. 16 cm
    c. 6 cm
    d. 20 cm

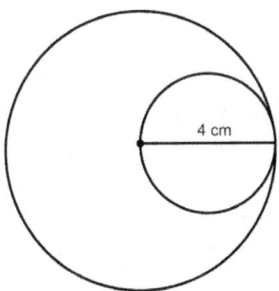

Note: Figure not drawn to scale

29. Assuming the diameter of the small circle is the radius of the larger circle, what is (area of large circle) - (area of small circle) in the figure above?

    a. 8π cm^2
    b. 10π cm^2
    c. 12π cm^2
    d. 16π cm^2

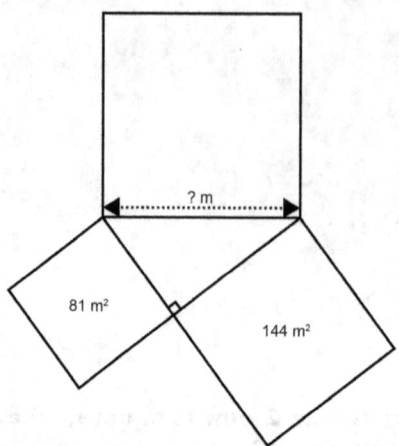

Note: Figure not drawn to scale

30. Assuming the shapes around the center right triangle are square, what is the length of each side of the indicated square above?

    a. 10
    b. 15
    c. 20
    d. 5

Answer Key

Decimals, Percent and Fractions

1. A
15/200 = X/100 = 1500 = 200X = 15 = 2X = 7.5%

2. C
Total no. of balls = 10, no. of yellow balls = 2, answer = 2/10 X 100 = 20%

3. B
10% of 300 = 30 and 50% of 20 = 10 so 30 + 10 = 40.

4. C
75% = 75/100 = 3/4

5. D
90% = 90/100 = 9/10

6. B
25% of 40 = 10 and 10 x 3 = 30

7. A
0.28 = 28/100 = 7/25

8. C
0.45 = 45/100 = 9/20

9. C
1/5 X 100 = 20%

10. B
4/20 X 100 = 1/5 X 100 = 20%

11. B
(Amount Spent) $420 + $3000 (Balance) = $3420

12. B
9.60/3.2 = 3

13. B
X = 7, so 3x = 3 x 7 = 21, 2x = 2 x 7 = 14, so 21 + 5 - 14 = 26 - 14 = 12. Be careful, to perform the operations in the correct order - multiplication first, then addition and subtraction.

14. C
There are two fractions containing x and the denominators are different. First, let us find a common denominator to simplify the expression. The least common multiplier of 4 and 7 is 28. Then,
7(x – 2) / 28 – 4(3x + 5) / 28 = - 3.28 / 28 ... Since both sides are written on the denominator 28 now, we can eliminate them:
7(x – 2) – 4(3x + 5) = – 84
7x – 14 – 12x – 20 = – 84
- 5x = - 84 + 14 + 20
- 5x = - 50
x = 50/5

x = 10

15. A
Multiply the first bracket and the second. x^2 - 3x + 7x -21= x^2 + 4x – 21

16. B
X > 12 – 3, = x > 9

17. C
The approximate answer to 5205 / 25 is 208.

EXPONENTS

18. A
3 x 3 x 3 x 3 = 81

19. C
(4 x 4 x 4) + (2 x 2 x 2 x 2) = 64 + 16 = 80

20. D

Mathematics 149

$2(5)^3 - (2)^3 = 2(125) - 8 = 250 - 8 = 242$

21. D
$X^3 \times X^2 = X^{3+2} = X^5$

22. A
Any value (except 0) raised to the power of 0 equals 1.

PROBABILITY

23. A
The probability that the 1st ball drawn is red = 4/11. The probability that the 2nd ball drawn is green = 5/10. The combined probability will then be 4/11 X 5/10 = 20/110 = 2/11.

24. B
Absent students = 83 – 72 = 11
Percentage of absent students = 11/83 = X/100
1100 = 83x
x = 1100/83
13.25 Reducing up to two significant digits it will be 13.

25. A
The chance of tossing a coin and getting heads will always be 1/2. How many times heads has been observed in the past does not affect the probability of heads in the future.

GEOMETRY

26. A
Point A represents the origin.

27. A
The diagonals of a square intersect at right angles, so each angle measures 90° Half of that angle will be 45°

28. B
We see that there is a square with side 2 cm and a rectangle adjacent to it, with one side 2 cm (common side with the square) and the other side 4 cm. The perimeter of a shape is found by summing up all sides surrounding the shape, not adding the ones inside the shape. Three 2 cm sides from the square, and two 4 cm sides and one 2 cm side from the

rectangle contribute the perimeter.

So, the perimeter of the shape is: 2 + 2 + 2 + 4 + 2 + 4 = 16 cm.

29. C

In the figure, we are given a large circle and a small circle inside it; with the diameter equal to the radius of the large one. The diameter of the small circle is 4 cm. This means that its radius is 2 cm. Since the diameter of the small circle is the radius of the large circle, the radius of the large circle is 4 cm. The area of a circle is calculated by: $πr^2$ where r is the radius.

Area of the small circle: $π(2)^2 = 4π$

Area of the large circle: $π(4)^2 = 16π$

The difference area is found by:

Area of the large circle - Area of the small circle = $16π - 4π = 12π$

30. B

We see that there are three squares forming a right triangle in the middle. Two of the squares have the areas 81 m² and 144 m². If we denote their sides a and b respectively:

$a^2 = 81$ and $b^2 = 144$. The length which is asked is the hypotenuse; a and b are the opposite and adjacent sides of the right angle. By using the Pythagorean Theorem, we can find the value of the asked side:

Pythagorean Theorem:

$(Hypotenuse)^2 = (Opposite\ Side)^2 + (Adjacent\ Side)^2$

$h^2 = a^2 + b^2$

$a^2 = 81$ and $b^2 = 144$ are given. So;

$h^2 = 81 + 144$

$h^2 = 225$

$h = 15$ m

Basic Math Video Tutorials

https://www.test-preparation.ca/math-videos/

Fraction Tips, Tricks and Shortcuts

When you are writing an exam, time is precious, so anything you can do to answer questions faster is a real advantage.

Here are some ideas, shortcuts, tips and tricks that can speed up answering fraction problems.

Remember that a fraction is just a number which names a portion of something. For instance, instead of having a whole pie, a fraction says you have a part of a pie--such as a half of one or a fourth of one.

Two numbers make up a fraction. The number on top is the numerator. The number on the bottom is the denominator.

To remember which is which, just remember that "denominator" and "down" both start with a "d." And the "downstairs" number is the denominator. So for instance, in ½, the numerator is 1, and the denominator (or "downstairs") number is 2.

Adding Fractions

It's easy to add two fractions if they have the same denominator. Just add the digits on top and leave the bottom one the same: 1/10 + 6/10 = 7/10.

It's the same with subtracting fractions with the same denominator: 7/10 - 6/10 = 1/10.

Adding and subtracting fractions with different denominators is a little more complicated.

First, you have to arrange the fractions so they have the same denominators.

The easiest way to do this is to multiply the denominators: For 2/5 + 1/2 multiply 5 by 2. Now you have a denominator of 10.

But now you have to change the top numbers too. Since you multiplied the 5 in 2/5 by 2, you also multiply the 2 by 2, to get 4. So the first fraction is now 4/10.

In the second fraction, you multiplied the denominator by 5, you have to multiply the numerator by 5 also, to get 5/10.

Now you have 4/10 + 5/10 and you can add 5 and 4 to get 9/10.

Simplest Form

To reduce a fraction to its simplest form, you have to arrange the numerator and denominator so the only common factor is 1.

Think of it this way:

Let's take an example: The fraction 2/10.

This is not reduced to its simplest terms because there is a number that will divide evenly into both: 2. We want to make it so that the only number that will divide evenly into both is 1.

Divide the top and bottom by 2 to get the new, reduced fraction - 1/5.

Multiplying Fractions

This is the easiest of all: Just multiply the two top numbers and then multiply the two bottom numbers.

Here is an example,

2/5 X 2/3

First, multiply the numerators: 2 X 2 = 4

then multiply the denominators: 5 X 3 = 15

Your answer is 4/15.

Dividing Fractions

Dividing fractions is easy if you remember a simple trick - first turn the second fraction upside down - then multiply!

Here is an example:

7/8 X 1/2

Turn the second fraction upside down:

7/8 X 2/1

then multiply:

(7 X 2) / (8 X 1) = 14/8

CONVERTING FRACTIONS TO DECIMALS

There are a couple of ways to convert fractions to decimals. The first, which is the fastest -- is to memorize some basic fraction facts.

1/100 is "one hundredth," expressed as a decimal, it's .01.

1/50 is "two hundredths," expressed as a decimal, it's .02.

1/25 is "one twenty-fifth" or "four hundredths," expressed as a decimal, it's .04.

1/20 is "one twentieth" or ""five hundredths," expressed as a decimal, it's .05.

1/10 is "one tenth," expressed as a decimal, it's .1.

1/8 is "one eighth," or "one hundred twenty-five thousandths," expressed as a decimal, it's .125.

1/5 is "one fifth," or "two tenths," expressed as a decimal, it's .2.

1/4 is "one fourth" or "twenty-five hundredths," expressed as a decimal, it's .25.

1/3 is "one third" or "thirty-three hundredths," expressed as a decimal, it's .33.

1/2 is "one half" or "five tenths," expressed as a decimal, it's .5.

3/4 is "three fourths," or "seventy-five hundredths," expressed as a decimal, it's .75.

Of course, if you're no good at memorization, another good technique for converting a fraction to a decimal is to manipulate it so that the fraction's denominator is 10, 100, 1000, or some other power of 10.

Here's an example: We'll start with three quarters. What is the first number in the 4 "times table" that you can multiply and get a multiple of 10? Can you multiply 4 by something to get 10? No. Can you multiply it by something to get 100? Yes! 4 X 25 is 100.

So multiply the numerator by 25, which is 75 over 100

We know fractions are really a division problem, and we also know that dividing by 100, means we move the decimal 2 places to the left.

So, 75 over 100 = .75

Lets try another example - Convert one fifth to a decimal.

First find a power of 10 that 5 goes into evenly, which is 2.

Multiply the numerator and denominator by 2, which is

two tenths.

Dividing 2 by 10 means we move the decimal place 1 place to the left.

So 1/5 = 0.5

Converting Fractions to Percent

Here is a quick method to convert fraction to percent and a strategy for answering on a multiple choice test that will save you valuable exam time.

First, remember that a fraction is a division problem: you're dividing the bottom number into the top.

Taking an example, convert 2/3 into percent.

The first method is to multiple the numerator by 100 and divide. So,

(2 X 100) / 2 = 100/3 = 66.66

Add a % sign and you have the answer, 66.66%

If you're doing these conversions on a multiple-choice test, here's an idea that might be even easier and faster. Let's say you have a fraction of 1/8 and you're asked to convert to percent.

Since we know that "percent" means hundredths, ask yourself what number we can multiply 8 by to get 100. Since there is no number, ask what number gets us close to 100.

That number is 12: 8 X 12 = 96. So it gets us a little less than 100. Now, whatever you do to the denominator, you have to do to the numerator. Let's multiply 1 X 12 and we get 12. However, since 96 is a little less than 100, we know that our answer will be a little MORE than 12%.

Look at the choices and eliminate the obvious wrong choices. So if your possible answers on the multiple-choice test are these:

a) 8.5% b) 19% c) 12.5% d) 25%

then we know the answer is c) 12.5%, because it's a little MORE than the 12 we got in our math problem above.

Here all the choices except choice C 12.5% can be eliminated.

You don't have to know the exact correct answer, just enough to estimate, then eliminate the obviously wrong answers.

This was an easy example to demonstrate the strategy, but don't be fooled! You probably won't get such an easy question on your exam. By estimating your answer quickly, then eliminating obviously incorrect choices immediately, you save precious exam time.

Decimal Tips, Tricks and Shortcuts

Converting Decimals to Fractions

Converting decimals to fractions is easy if you say it the right way! If you say "point one" or "point 25," you'll have trouble.

But if you say, "one tenth" and "twenty-five hundredths," then you have already solved it! That's because, if you know your fractions, you know that "one tenth" looks like this: 1/10. And "twenty-five hundredths" looks like this: 25/100.

Even if you have digits before the decimal, such as 3.4, learning how to say the word will help you with the conversion into a fraction. It's not "three point four," it's "three and four tenths." Knowing this, you know that the fraction which looks like "three and four tenths" is 3 4/10.

The conversion is not complete until you reduce the fraction to its lowest terms: It's not 25/100, but 1/4.

Converting Decimals to Percent

Changing a decimal to a percent is easy if you remember one thing: multiply by 100.

For example, if you start with .45, simply multiply it by 100 for 45. Then add the % sign to the end - 45%.

Think of it this way: take out the decimal point, add a percent sign on the opposite side. In other words, the decimal on the left is replaced by the % on the right.

It doesn't work quite that easily if the decimal is in the middle of the number. For example, 3.7. Here, take out the decimal in the middle and replace it with a 0 % at the end.

So 3.7 converted to decimal is 370%.

Percent Tips, Tricks and Shortcuts

Percent problems are not nearly as scary as they appear, if you remember this neat trick:

Draw a cross as in:

Portion	Percent
Whole	100

In the upper left, write PORTION. In the bottom left write WHOLE. In the top right, write PERCENT and in the bottom right, write 100. Whatever your problem is, you will leave blank the unknown, and fill in the other four parts. For example, let's suppose your problem is: Find 10% of 50. Since we know the 10% part, we put 10 in the percent corner. Since the whole number in our problem is 50, we put that in the corner marked whole. You always put 100 underneath the percent, so we leave it as is, which leaves only the top left corner blank. This is where we'll put our answer. Now simply multiply the two corner numbers that are NOT 100. Here, it's 10 X 50. That gives us 500. Now divide this by the remaining corner, or 100, to get a final answer of 5. 5 is the number that goes in the upper-left corner, and is your final solution.

Another hint to remember: Percents are the same thing as hundredths in decimals. So .45 is the same as 45 hundredths or 45 percent.

Converting Percents to Decimals

Percents are just a type of decimal, so it should be no surprise that converting between the two is actually fairly simple. Here are a few tricks and shortcuts to keep in mind:

- Remember that percent literally means "per 100" or "for every 100." So when you speak of 30% you're saying 30 for every 100 or the fraction 30/100. In basic math, you learned that fractions that have 10 or 100 as the denominator can easily be turned to a decimal. 30/100 is thirty hundredths, or expressed as a decimal, .30.
- Another way to look at it: To convert a percent to a decimal, simply divide the number by 100. So for instance, if the percent is 47%, divide 47 by 100. The result will be .47. Get rid of the % mark and you're done.
- Remember that the easiest way of dividing by 100 is by moving your decimal two spots to the left.

Converting Percents to Fractions

Converting percents to fractions is easy. After all, a percent is just a type of fraction; it tells you what part of 100 that you're talking about. Here are some simple ideas for making the conversion from a percent to a fraction:

- If the percent is a whole number -- say 34% -- then simply write a fraction with 100 as the denominator (the bottom number). Then put the percentage itself on top. So 34% becomes 34/100.
- Now reduce as you would reduce any percent. In this case, by dividing 2 into 34 and 2 into 100, you get 17/50.
- If your percent is not a whole number -- say 3.4% --then convert it to a decimal expressed as hundredths. 3.4 is the same as 3.40 (or 3 and forty hundredths). Now ask yourself how you would express "three and forty hundredths" as a fraction. It would, of course, be 3 40/100. Reduce this and it becomes 3 2/5.

EXPONENTS – A QUICK TUTORIAL

Exponents seem like advanced math to most—like some mysterious code with a complicated meaning. In fact, though, an exponent is just short hand for saying that you're multiplying a number by itself two or more times. For instance, instead of saying that you're multiplying 5 x 5 x 5, you can show that you're multiplying 5 by itself 3 times if you just write 5^3. We usually say this as "five to the third power" or "five to the power of three." In this example, the raised 3 is an "exponent," while the 5 is the "base." You can even use exponents with fractions. For instance, $1/2^3$ means you're multiplying 1/2 x 1/2 x 1/2. (The answer is 1/8). Some other helpful hints for working with exponents:

- Here's how to do basic multiplication of exponents. If you have the same number with a different exponent (For instance 5^3 X 5^2) just add the exponents and multiply the bases as usual. The answer, then, is 25^5.
- This doesn't work, though, if the bases are different. For instance, in 5^3 X 3^2 we simply have to do the math the long way to figure out the final solution: 5 x 5 x 5, multiplying that result times the result for 3 X 3. (The answer is 1125).
- Looking at it from the opposite side, to divide two exponents with the same base (or bottom number), subtract the smaller exponent from the larger one. If we were dividing the problem above, we would subtract the 2 from the 3 to get 1. 5 to the power of 1 is simply 5.
- One time when thinking of exponents as merely multiplication doesn't work is when the raised number is zero. Any number raised to the "zeroth" power is 1 (Not, as we tend to think, zero).

Number (x)	x^2	x^3
1	1	1
2	4	8
3	9	27
4	16	64
5	25	125
6	36	216
7	49	343
8	64	512
9	81	729
10	100	1000
11	121	1331
12	144	1728
13	169	2197
14	196	2744
15	225	3375
16	256	4096

The time allowed on the math portion of a standardized test is typically so short that there's no room for error. You have to be fast and accurate.

Math strategy is very helpful, but nothing beats knowing your stuff! Make sure that you have learned all the important formulas that will be used.

If you don't know the formulas, strategy won't help you.

How to Answer Basic Math Questions - the Basics

First, read the problem, but not the answers.

Work through the problem first and come up with your own answers. Hopefully, you should find your answer among the choices.

If no answer matches the one you got, re-check your math, but this time, use a different method. In math, there are different ways to solve a problem.

Math Multiple Choice Strategy

The two strategies for working with basic math multiple choice are Estimation and Elimination.

Estimation is just as it sounds - try to estimate an approximate answer first. Then look at the choices.

Elimination is probably the most powerful strategy for answering multiple choice.

Eliminate obviously incorrect answers and narrowing the possible choices.

Here are a few basic math examples of how this works.

Solve 2/3 + 5/12

  a. 9/17
  b. 3/11
  c. 7/12
  d. 1 1/12

First estimate the answer. 2/3 is more than half and 5/12 is about half, so the answer is going to be very close to 1.

Next, Eliminate. Choice A is about 1/2 and can be eliminated, choice B is very small, less than 1/2 and can be eliminated. Choice C is close to 1/2 and can be eliminated. Leaving only choice D, which is just over 1.

Work through the solution, find a common denominator and add. The correct answer is 1 1/12, so Choice D is correct.

Let's look at another example:

Solve 4/5 – 2/3

    a. 2/2
    b. 2/13
    c. 1
    d. 2/15

First, quickly estimate the answer. 4/5 is very close to 1, and 2/3 more than half, so the answer is going to be less than 1/2.

Choice A can be eliminated right away, because it is 1. Choice C can be eliminated for the same reason.

Next, look at the denominators. Since 5 and 3 don't go into 13, choice B can be eliminated as well.

That leaves choice D. Checking the answer, the common denominator will be 15. So the answer is 2/15 and choice D is correct.

FRACTIONS SHORTCUT - CANCELLING OUT.

In any operation with fractions, if the numerator of one fractions has a common multiple with the denominator of the other, you can cancel out. This saves time, and simplifies the problem quickly, making it easier to manage.

Solve 2/15 ÷ 4/5

    a. 6/65

    b. 6/75

    c. 5/12

    d. 1/6

To divide fractions, we multiply the first fraction with the inverse of the second fraction. Therefore we have 2/15 x 5/4. The numerator of the first fraction, 2, shares a multiple with the denominator of the second fraction, 4, which is 2. These cancel out, which gives, 1/3 x 1/2 = 1/6

Cancelling out solved the questions very quickly, but we can still use multiple choice strategies to answer.

Choice B can be eliminated because 75 is too large a denominator. Choice C can be eliminated because 5 and 15 don't go into 12.

Choice D is correct.

Decimal Multiple Choice Strategy and Shortcuts.

Multiplying decimals gives a very quick way to estimate and eliminate choices. Anytime that you multiply decimals, it is going to give an answer with the same number of decimal places as the combined operands.

So for example,

2.38 X 1.2 will produce a number with three places of decimal, which is 2.856.

Here are a few examples with step-by-step explanation:

Solve 2.06 x 1.2

    a. 24.82

    b. 2.482

    c. 24.72

    d. 2.472

This is a simple question, but even before you start calculating, you can eliminate several choices. When multiplying decimals, there will always be as many numbers behind the decimal place in the answer as the sum of the ones in the initial problem, so choices A and C can be eliminated.

The correct answer is D: 2.06 x 1.2 = 2.472

Solve 20.0 ÷ 2.5

    a. 12.05

    b. 9.25

    c. 8.3

    d. 8

First estimate the answer to be around 10, and eliminate choice A. And since it'd also be an even number, you can eliminate Choices B and C, leaving only choice D.

The correct answer is choice D: 20.0 ÷ 2.5 = 8

How to Solve Word Problems

Do you know what the biggest tip for solving word problems is?

Practice regularly and systematically.

Sounds simple and easy right? Yes it is, and yes it really does work.

Word problems are a way of thinking and require you to translate a real-world problem into mathematical terms.

Some math teachers say that learning how to think mathematically is the main reason for teaching word problems.

So what does that mean?

Studying word problems and math in general requires a logical and mathematical frame of mind. The only way you can get this is by practicing regularly, which means every day.

It is critical that you practice word problems every day for the 5 days before the exam as the absolute minimum.

If you practice and miss a day, you have lost the mathematical frame of mind and the benefit of your previous practice is gone. You must start all over again.

Everything is important.

All the information given in the problem has some purpose. There is no unnecessary information! Word problems are typically around 50 words in 2 or 3 sentences.

Often, the relationships are complicated. To explain everything, every word counts.

Make sure that you use every piece of information.

7 STEPS TO SOLVING WORD PROBLEMS

Step 1 – Read through the problem at least three times. The first reading should be a quick scan, and the next two readings should be done slowly to find answers to these questions:

> What does the problem ask? (Usually located at the end)

Mark all information and underline all important words or phrases.

Step 2 – Draw a picture. Use arrows, circles, lines, whatever works for you. This makes the problem real.

A favorite word problem is something like, 1 train leaves Station A travelling at 100 km/hr and another train leaves Station B travelling at 60 km/hr. ...

Draw a line, the two stations, and the two trains at either end.

Depending on the question, make a table with a blank portion to show information you don't know.

Step 3 – Assign a single letter to represent each unknown.

You may want to note the unknown that each letter represents so you don't get confused.

Step 4 – Translate the information into an equation.

Remember that the main problem with word problems is that they are not expressed in regular math equations. Your ability to identify correctly the variables and translate the information into an equation determines your ability to solve the problem.

Step 5 – Check the equation to see if it looks like regular equations that you are used to seeing and whether it looks sensible.

Does the equation appear to represent the information in the question? Take note that you may need to rewrite some formulas needed to solve the word problem equation.

Step 6 – Use algebra rules to solve the equation.

Simplify each side of the equation by removing parentheses and combining like terms.

Use addition or subtraction to isolate the variable term on one side of the equation. If a number crosses to the other side of the equation, the sign changes to the opposite -- for example positive to negative.

Use multiplication or division to solve for the variable. What you to once side of the equation you must do for the other.

Where there are multiple unknowns you will need to use elimination or substitution methods to resolve all the equations.

Step 7 – Check your final answers to see if they make sense with the information given in the problem.

For example, if the word problem involves a discount, the final price should be less or if a product was taxed then the final answer has to cost more.

TYPES OF WORD PROBLEMS

Word problems can be classified into 12 types. Below are examples of each type with a complete solution. Some types of word problems can be solved quickly using multiple choice strategies and some cannot. Always look for ways to estimate the answer and then eliminate choices.

1. Age

A girl is 10 years older than her brother. By next year, she will be twice the age of her brother. What are their ages now?

    a. 25, 15
    b. 19, 9
    c. 21, 11
    d. 29, 19

Solution: B

We will assume that the girl's age is "a" and her brother's age is "b." This means that based on the information in the first sentence,
$a = 10 + b$

Next year, she will be twice her brother's age, which gives, $a + 1 = 2(b + 1)$

We need to solve for one unknown factor and then use the answer to solve for the other. To do this we substitute the value of "a" from the first equation into the second equation. This gives

$10 + b + 1 = 2b + 2$
$11 + b = 2b + 2$
$11 - 2 = 2b - b$
$b = 9$

$9 = b$ this means that her brother is 9 years old. Solving for the girl's age in the first equation gives $a = 10 + 9$. $a = 19$ the girl is aged 19. So, the girl is aged 19 and the boy is 9

2. Distance or speed

Two boats travel down a river towards the same destination, starting at the same time. One boat is traveling at 52 km/hr, and the other boat at 43 km/hr. How far apart will they be after 40 minutes?

    a. 46.67 km

    b. 19.23 km

    c. 6.04 km

    d. 14.39 km

Solution: C

After 40 minutes, the first boat will have traveled = 52 km/hr x 40 minutes/60 minutes = 34.66 km
After 40 minutes, the second boat will have traveled = 43 km/hr x 40/60 minutes = 28.66 km
Difference between the two boats will be 34.66 km – 28.66 km = 6 km.

Multiple Choice Strategy

First estimate the answer. The first boat is travelling 9 km. faster than the second, for 40 minutes, which is 2/3 of an hour. 2/3 of 9 = 6, as a rough guess of the distance apart.

Choices A, B and D can be eliminated right away.

3. Ratio

The instructions in a cookbook state that 700 grams of flour must be mixed in 100 ml of water, and 0.90 grams of salt added. A cook however has just 325 grams of flour. What is the quantity of water and salt that he should use?

    a. 0.41 grams and 46.4 ml
    b. 0.45 grams and 49.3 ml
    c. 0.39 grams and 39.8 ml
    d. 0.25 grams and 40.1 ml

Solution: A

The Cookbook states 700 grams of flour, but the cook only has 325. The first step is to determine the percentage of flour he has 325/700 x 100 = 46.4%
That means that 46.4% of all other items must also be used.
46.4% of 100 = 46.4 ml of water
46.4% of 0.90 = 0.41 grams of salt.

Multiple Choice Strategy

The recipe calls for 700 grams of flour but the cook only has 325, which is just less than half, the quantity of water and salt are going to be about half.

Choices C and D can be eliminated right away. Choice B is very close so be careful. Looking closely at Choice B, it is exactly half, and since 325 is slightly less than half of 700, it can't be correct.

Choice A is correct.

4. Percent

An agent received $6,685 as his commission for selling a property. If his commission was 13% of the selling price, how much was the property?

    a. $68,825
    b. $121,850
    c. $49,025
    d. $51,423

Solution: D

Let's assume that the property price is x
That means from the information given, 13% of x = 6,685
Solve for x,
x = 6685 x 100/13 = $51,423

Multiple Choice Strategy

The commission, 13%, is just over 10%, which is easier to work with. Round up $6685 to $6700, and multiple by 10 for an approximate answer. 10 X 6700 = $67,000. You can do this in your head. Choice B is much too big and can be eliminated. Choice C is too small and can be eliminated. Choices A and D are left and good possibilities.

Do the calculations to make the final choice.

5. Sales & Profit

A store owner buys merchandise for $21,045. He transports them for $3,905 and pays his staff $1,450 to stock the merchandise on his shelves. If he does not incur further costs, how much does he need to sell the items to make $5,000 profit?

    a. $32,500
    b. $29,350
    c. $32,400
    d. $31,400

Solution: D

Total cost of the items is $21,045 + $3,905 + $1,450 = $26,400
Total cost is now $26,400 + $5000 profit = $31,400

Multiple Choice Strategy

Round off and add the numbers up in your head quickly.
21,000 + 4,000 + 1500 = 26500. Add in 5000 profit for a total of 31500.

Choice B is too small and can be eliminated. Choices C and A are too large and can be eliminated.

6. Tax/Income

A woman earns $42,000 per month and pays 5% tax on her monthly income. If the Government increases her monthly taxes by $1,500, what is her income after tax?

    a. $38,400
    b. $36,050
    c. $40,500
    d. $39, 500

Solution: A

Initial tax on income was 5/100 x 42,000 = $2,100
$1,500 was added to the tax to give $2,100 + 1,500 = $3,600
Income after tax is $42,000 - $3,600 = $38,400

7. Simple Interest Word Problems

Simple interest is one type of interest problems. There are always four variables of any simple interest equation. With simple interest, you would be given three of these variables and be asked to solve for one unknown variable. With more complex interest problems, you would have to solve for multiple variables.

The four variables of simple interest are:

Mathematics

P – Principal which refers to the original amount of money put in the account
I – Interest or the amount of money earned as interest
r – Rate or interest rate. This MUST ALWAYS be in decimal format and not in percentage
t – Time or the amount of time the money is kept in the account to earn interest

The formula for simple interest is I = P x r x t

Example 1

A customer deposits $1,000 in a savings account with a bank that offers 2% interest. How much interest will be earned after 4 years?
For this problem, there are 3 variables as expected.

P = $1,000
t = 4 years
r = 2%
I = ?

Before we can begin solving for I using the simple interest formula, we need to first convert the rate from percentage to decimal.

2% = 2/100 = 0.02

Now we can use the formula: I = P x r x t

I = 1,000 x 0.02 x 4 = 80
This means that the $1,000 would have earned an interest of $80 after 4 years. The total in the account after 4 years will thus be principal + interest earned, or 1,000 + 80 = $1,080

Example 2

Sandra deposits $1400 in a savings account with a bank at 5% interest. How long will she have to leave the money in the bank to earn $420 as interest to buy a second-hand car?

In this example, the given information is:
I = $420

P = $1,400
r - 5%
t - ?
As usual, first we convert the rate from percentage to decimal
5% = 5/100 = 0.05

Next, we plug in the variables we know into the simple interest formula - I = P x r x t

420 = 1,400 x 0.05 x t
420 = 70 x t
420 = 70t
t = 420/70
t = 6

Sandra will have to leave her $1,400 in the bank for 6 years to earn her an interest of $420 at a rate of 5%.

Other important simple interest formula to remember

To use this formula below, do not convert r (rate) to decimal.

P = 100 x interest/ r x t
r = 100 x interest/p x t
t = 100 x interest/ p x r

8. Averaging

The average weight of 10 books is 54 grams. 2 more books were added and the average weight became 55.4. If one of the 2 new books added weighed 62.8 g, what is the weight of the other?

    a. 44.7 g
    b. 67.4 g
    c. 62 g
    d. 52 g

Solution: C

Total weight of 10 books with average 54 grams will be = 10 × 54 = 540 g

Total weight of 12 books with average 55.4 will be = 55.4 × 12 = 664.8 g
So total weight of the remaining 2 will be= 664.8 − 540 = 124.8 g
If one weighs 62.8, the weight of the other will be= 124.8 g − 62.8 g = 62 g

Multiple Choice Strategy

Averaging problems can be estimated by looking at which direction the average goes. If additional items are added and the average goes up, the new items much be greater than the average. If the average goes down after new items are added, the new items must be less than the average.

Here, the average is 54 grams and 2 books are added which increases the average to 55.4, so the new books must weight more than 54 grams.
Choices A and D can be eliminated right away.

9. Probability

A bag contains 15 marbles of various colors. If 3 marbles are white, 5 are red and the rest are black, what is the probability of randomly picking out a black marble from the bag?

   a. 7/15
   b. 3/15
   c. 1/5
   d. 4/15

Solution: A

Total marbles = 15
Number of black marbles = 15 − (3 + 5) = 7
Probability of picking out a black marble = 7/15

10. Two Variables

A company paid a total of $2850 to book for 6 single rooms and 4 double rooms in a hotel for one night. Another company paid $3185 to book for 13 single rooms for one night in the same hotel. What is the cost for single and double rooms in that hotel?

    a. single= $250 and double = $345
    b. single= $254 and double = $350
    c. single = $245 and double = $305
    d. single = $245 and double = $345

Solution: D

We can determine the price of single rooms from the information given of the second company. 13 single rooms = 3185.
One single room = 3185 / 13 = 245
The first company paid for 6 single rooms at $245. 245 x 6 = $1470
Total amount paid for 4 double rooms by first company = $2850 - $1470 = $1380
Cost per double room = 1380 / 4 = $345

11. Geometry

The length of a rectangle is 5 in. more than its width. The perimeter of the rectangle is 26 in. What is the width and length of the rectangle?

    a. width = 6 inches, Length = 9 inches
    b. width = 4 inches, Length = 9 inches
    c. width =4 inches, Length = 5 inches
    d. width = 6 inches, Length = 11 inches

Solution: B

Formula for perimeter of a rectangle is 2(L + W)
p=26, so 2(L+W) = p
The length is 5 inches more than the width, so
2(w+5) + 2w = 26
2w + 10 + 2w = 26

$2w + 2w = 26 - 10$
$4w = 16$

$W = 16/4 = 4$ inches

L is 5 inches more than w, so $L = 5 + 4 = 9$ inches.

12. Totals and fractions

A basket contains 125 oranges, mangos and apples. If 3/5 of the fruits in the basket are mangos and only 2/5 of the mangos are ripe, how many ripe mangos are there in the basket?

    a. 30
    b. 68
    c. 55
    d. 47

Solution: A
Number of mangos in the basket is $3/5 \times 125 = 75$
Number of ripe mangos = $2/5 \times 75 = 30$

ALGEBRAIC EQUATIONS

Algebra is a basic form of mathematics designed to define unknown quantities called variables. Variables in algebra are represented by letters, often x, y and z or a, b and c, and they are placed in equations alongside known quantities. An algebraic equation can be as simple as $2x=6$ where simple division can tell us that $x=6/2$ or $x = 3$. Equations can also have variables on both sides such as $2x+3=8x$. For this equation, we need to take more steps. First, subtracting 2x from both sides we get the equation $3=6x$. From there it is again a simple matter of division to show that $x=.5$. The point of an equation is that it demonstrates that two distinct pieces of information have the same value. (It equates them.) Even though we do not know what $2x+3$ is or what $8x$ is, we at least know that they are the same.

There are three types of equalities in algebra. There are reflexive equalities that say $x=x$. There are symmetric equalities that say that if $x=y$ then $y=x$ as well. And there are transitive equalities that say that if $x=y$ and $y=z$ then $x=z$.

The definite number next to the variable in each equation is called its coefficient. A variable can always be thought of as having a coefficient; if there is no number next to it, the coefficient equals 1, and if it has a negative sign in front of it, the coefficient equals -1.

Often, algebra is presented as word problems and it is up to you to figure out the equation. For instance, a question might describe a hockey team that has 6 wins, 3 losses in regulation time and 1 loss in overtime over their last 10 games. It will then tell you that the team has 13 points (awarded for wins and overtime losses to organize the league's standings) in their last 10 games and ask, given that a regulation loss earns a team 0 points: How many points is a win worth? How many is an overtime loss worth?

This question will give you the variables x = a win, y = a regulation loss and z = an overtime loss, from which you can derive the equation $6x+3y+1z=13$. Since you already know that $y=0$ points, you can rewrite the equation as $6x+z=13$. Now we have a two variable or polynomial equation to solve. First, we need to find a way to rewrite it so that there is only one variable in the equation. If we solve for x we get the equation $6x=13-1z$ which can be simplified to $x=2z$. We can then plug that into the original equation and get $6(2z)+z=13$ or $13z=13$ or $z=1$. Now we know two variables that we can use to solve for x and we can write the equation $6x+1=13$ or $x=2$. Thus, we can tell that in hockey teams get 2 points for each regulation win ($x=2$) and 1 point for each overtime win ($z=1$).

This is a highly simplified example of algebra, but the same process works with any basic mathematical function provided you follow the order of operations. The order of operations is the order in which you have to perform each mathematical function to get the correct answer. Following the order of operations is important because while some operations can be done in any order:

(1+2)+3 = 3+3 = 6 is the same as (2+3)+1 = 5+1 = 6

others cannot:

(10-2)/4 = 8/4 = 2 is not the same as (10/4)-2 = 2.5-2 = .5

Doing the operations in any order you want can give you very incorrect results.

The order of operations goes: parentheses, exponents, multiplication, division, addition, subtraction. It can be remembered through the acronym Please Excuse My Dear Aunt Sally.

Algebra Solutions - Video Tutorial

https://www.test-preparation.ca/algebra-practice-questions/

RATIOS

In mathematics, a ratio is a relationship between two numbers of the same kind[1] (e.g., objects, persons, students, spoonfuls, units of whatever identical dimension), usually expressed as "a to b" or a:b, sometimes expressed arithmetically as a dimensionless quotient of the two[2] which explicitly shows how many times the first number contains the second (not necessarily an integer).[3] In layman's terms a ratio represents, simply, for every amount of one thing, how much there is of another thing. For example, suppose I have 10 pairs of socks for every pair of shoes then the ratio of shoes:socks would be 1:10 and the ratio of socks:shoes would be 10:1.

Notation and terminology

The ratio of numbers A and B can be expressed as:[4]
the ratio of A to B
A is to B

A:B

A rational number which is the quotient of A divided by B The numbers A and B are sometimes called terms with A being the antecedent and B being the consequent.

The proportion expressing the equality of the ratios A:B and C:D is written A:B=C:D or A:B::C:D. this latter form, when spoken or written in the English language, is often expressed as
A is to B as C is to D.

Again, A, B, C, D are called the terms of the proportion. A and D are called the extremes, and B and C are called the means. The equality of three or more proportions is called a continued proportion.[5]
Ratios are sometimes used with three or more terms. The dimensions of a two by four that is ten inches long are 2:4:10.

Examples

The quantities being compared in a ratio might be physical quantities such as speed or length, or numbers of objects, or amounts of particular substances. A common example of the last case is the weight ratio of water to cement used in concrete, which is commonly stated as 1:4. This means that the weight of cement used is four times the weight of water used. It does not say anything about the total amounts of cement and water used, nor the amount of concrete being made. Equivalently it could be said that the ratio of cement to water is 4:1, that there is 4 times as much cement as water, or that there is a quarter (1/4) as much water as cement..
Older televisions have a 4:3 "aspect ratio," which means that the width is 4/3 of the height; modern widescreen TVs have a 16:9 aspect ratio.

Fractional

If there are 2 oranges and 3 apples, the ratio of oranges to apples is 2:3, and the ratio of oranges to the total number of pieces of fruit is 2:5. These ratios can also be expressed in fraction form: there are 2/3 as many oranges as apples, and 2/5 of the pieces of fruit are oranges. If orange juice concentrate is to be diluted with water in the ratio 1:4, then one part of concentrate is mixed with four parts of water, giving five parts total; the amount of orange juice concentrate is 1/4 the amount of water, while the amount of orange juice concentrate is 1/5 of the total liquid. In both ratios and fractions, it is important to be clear what is being compared to what.

Number of terms

In general, when comparing the quantities of a two-quantity ratio, this can be expressed as a fraction derived from the ratio. For example, in a ratio of 2:3, the amount/size/volume/number of the first quantity will be that of the second quantity. This pattern also works with ratios with more than two terms. However, a ratio with more than two terms cannot be completely converted into a single fraction; a single fraction represents only one part of the ratio since a fraction can only compare two numbers. If the ratio deals with objects or amounts of objects, this is often expressed as "for every two parts of the first quantity there are three parts of the second quantity."

Percentage ratio

If we multiply all quantities involved in a ratio by the same number, the ratio remains valid. For example, a ratio of 3:2 is the same as 12:8. It is usual either to reduce terms to the lowest common denominator, or to express them in parts per hundred (percent).

If a mixture contains substances A, B, C & D in the ratio 5:9:4:2 then there are 5 parts of A for every 9 parts of B, 4 parts of C and 2 parts of D. As 5+9+4+2=20, the total mixture contains 5/20 of A (5 parts out of 20), 9/20 of B, 4/20 of C, and 2/20 of D. If we divide all numbers by the total and multiply by 100, this is converted to percentages: 25% A, 45% B, 20% C, and 10% D (equivalent to writing the ratio as 25:45:20:10).

PROPORTION

If the two or more ratio quantities encompass all the quantities in a particular situation, for example two apples and three oranges in a fruit basket containing no other types of fruit, it could be said that "the whole" contains five parts, made up of two parts apples and three parts oranges. In this case, or 40% of the whole are apples or 60% of the whole are oranges. This comparison of a specific quantity to "the whole" is sometimes called a proportion. Proportions are sometimes expressed as percentages as demonstrated above.

REDUCTION

Note that ratios can be reduced (as fractions are) by dividing each quantity by the common factors of all the quantities. This is often called "cancelling." As for fractions, the simplest form is considered to be that in which the numbers in the ratio are the smallest possible integers.

Thus, the ratio 40:60 may be considered equivalent in meaning to the ratio 2:3 within contexts concerned only with relative quantities.

Mathematically, we write: "40:60" = "2:3" (dividing both quantities by 20).
Grammatically, we would say, "40 to 60 equals 2 to 3."
An alternative representation is: "40:60::2:3"
Grammatically, we would say, "40 is to 60 as 2 is to 3."
A ratio that has integers for both quantities and that cannot be reduced any farther (using integers) is said to be in simplest form or lowest terms.
Sometimes it is useful to write a ratio in the form 1:n or n:1 to enable comparisons of different ratios.

For example, the ratio 4:5 can be written as 1:1.25 (dividing both sides by 4)

Alternately, 4:5 can be written as 0.8:1 (dividing both sides by 5)

Where the context makes the meaning clear, a ratio in this form is sometimes written without the 1 and the colon, though, mathematically, this makes it a factor or multiplier.

CARTESIAN PLANE, COORDINATE PLANE AND COORDINATE GRID

To locate points and draw lines and curves, we use the coordinate plane. It also called Cartesian coordinate plane. It is a two-dimensional surface with a coordinate grid in it, which helps us to count the units. For the counting of those units, we use x-axis (horizontal scale) and y-axis (vertical scale).

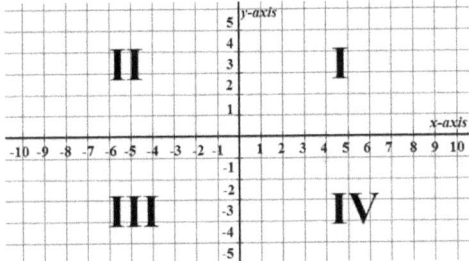

The whole system is called a coordinate system which is divided into 4 parts, called quadrants. The quadrant where all numbers are positive is the 1st quadrant (I), and if we go counterclockwise, we mark all 4 quadrants.

The location of a dot in the coordinate system is represented by coordinates. Coordinates are represented as a pair of numbers, where the 1st number is located on the x-axis and the 2nd number is located on the y-axis. So, if a dot A has coordinates a and b, then we write:

A=(a,b)   or   A(a,b)

The point where x-axis and y-axis intersect is called an origin. The origin is the point from which we measure the distance along the x and y axes.

In the Cartesian coordinate system we can calculate the distance between 2 given points. If we have dots with coordinates:

A=(a,b)
B=(c,d)

Then the distance d between A and B can be calculated by the following formula:

$$d = \sqrt{(c-a)^2 + (d-b)^2}$$

Cartesian coordinate system is used for the drawing of 2-dimentional shapes, and is also commonly used for functions.

Example:

Draw the function   y = (1 - x)/2

To draw a linear function, we need at least 2 points.
If we put that x=0 then value for y would be:

$$y = \frac{1-x}{2} = \frac{1-0}{2} = \frac{1}{2}$$

We found the 1st point, let's name it A, with following coordinates:

A = (0,1/2)

To find the 2nd point, we can put that x=1. In this case, the value for y would be:

$$y = \frac{1-x}{2} = \frac{1-1}{2} = \frac{0}{2} = 0$$

If we denote the 2nd point with B, then the coordinates for this point are:

B=(1,0)

Since we have 2 points necessary for the function, we find them in the coordinate system and we connect them with a line that represents the function,

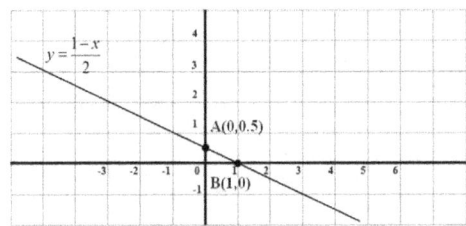

PERIMETER AREA AND VOLUME

Perimeter and Area (2-dimentional shapes)

Perimeter of a shape determines the length around that shape, while the area includes the space inside the shape.

Rectangle:

$P = 2a + 2b$
$A = ab$

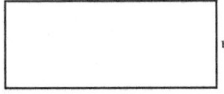

Square

$P = 4a$
$A = a^2$

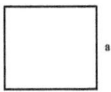

Parallelogram

$P = 2a + 2b$
$A = ah_a = bh_b$

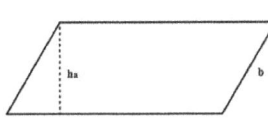

Rhombus

$P = 4a$

$A = ah = \dfrac{d_1 d_2}{2}$

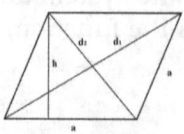

Triangle

$P = a + b + c$

$A = \dfrac{ah_a}{2} = \dfrac{bh_b}{2} = \dfrac{ch_c}{2}$

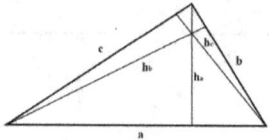

Equilateral Triangle

$P = 3a$

$A = \dfrac{a^2 \sqrt{3}}{4}$

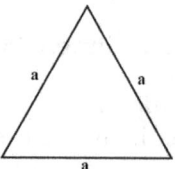

Trapezoid

$P = a + b + c + d$

$A = \dfrac{a+b}{2} h$

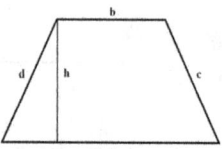

Circle

$P = 2r\pi$

$A = r^2 \pi$

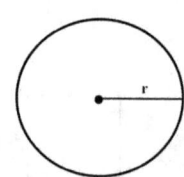

Area and Volume (3-dimentional shapes)

To calculate the area of a 3-dimentional shape, we calculate the areas of all sides and then we add them all.

To find the volume of a 3-dimentional shape, we multiply the area of the base (B) and the height (H) of the 3-dimentional shape.

$$V = BH$$

In case of a pyramid and a cone, the volume would be divided by 3.

$$V = BH/3$$

Here are some of the 3-dimentional shapes with formulas for their area and volume:

Cuboids

$A = 2(ab + bc + ac)$
$V = abc$

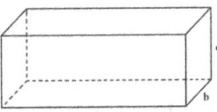

Cube

$A = 6a^2$
$V = a^3$

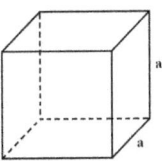

Pyramid

$A = ab + ah_a + bh_b$
$V = \dfrac{abH}{3}$

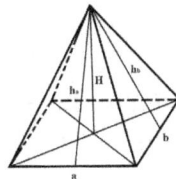

Cylinder

$A = 2r^2\pi + 2r\pi H$

$V = r^2\pi H$

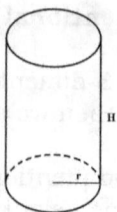

Cone

$A = (r+s)r\pi$

$V = \dfrac{r^2\pi H}{3}$

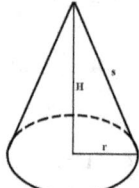

PYTHAGOREAN GEOMETRY

If we have a right triangle ABC, where its sides (legs) are a and b and c is a hypotenuse (the side opposite the right angle), then we can establish a relationship between these sides using the following formula:

$c^2 = a^2 + b^2$

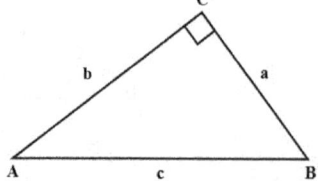

This formula is proven in the Pythagorean Theorem. There are many proofs of this theorem, but we'll look at just one geometrical proof:

If we draw squares on the right triangle's sides, then the area of the square upon the hypotenuse is equal to the sum of the areas of the squares that are upon other two sides of the triangle. Since the areas of these squares are a², b² and c², that is how we got the formula above.

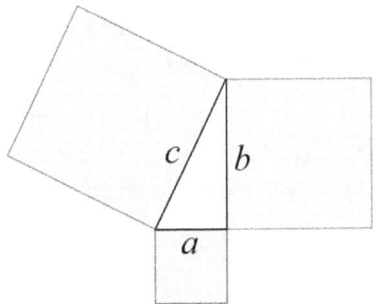

One of the famous right triangles is one with sides 3, 4 and 5. And we can see here that:

3² + 4² = 5²
9 + 16 = 25
25 = 25

Example Problem:

The isosceles triangle ABC has a perimeter of 18 centimeters, and the difference between its base and legs is 3 centimeters. Find the height of this triangle.

We write the information we have about triangle ABC and we draw a picture of it for better understanding of the relation

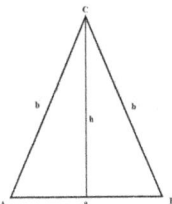

between its elements:

P=18 cm
a - b = 3 cm
h=?

We use the formula for the perimeter of the isosceles triangle, since that is what is given to us:
P = a + 2b = 18 cm

Notice that we have 2 equations with 2 variables, so we can solve it as a system of equations:

a + 2b = 18
a − b = 3 / a + 2b = 18
2a − 2b = 6 / a + 2b + 2a − 2b = 18 + 6
3a = 24
a = 24/3 = 8 cm

Now we go back to find b:
a - b = 3
8 - b = 3
b = 8 - 3
b = 5 cm

Using Pythagorean Theorem, we can find the height using a and b, because the height falls on the side a at the right angle. Notice that height cuts side a exactly in half, and that's why we use in the formula a/2. In this case, b is our hypotenuse, so we have:

$b^2 = (a/2)^2 + h^2$
$h^2 = b^2 - (a/2)^2$
$h^2 = 5^2 - (8/2)^2$
$h^2 = 5^2 - (8/2)^2$
$h^2 = 25 - 4^2$
$h^2 = 26 - 16$
$h^2 = 9$
h = 3 cm.

SCALE DRAWINGS

To draw some object accurately, but we can't draw it in its real size because it's either too small or too big, we use then scale drawing. It is called 'scale' because we use different scale – that is how much is the drawing of an object is bigger or smaller than its original size.

Scale drawing is written as x:y, where x represents the drawn size of the object and y represents the actual size of the object, actually how many times the drawn object is smaller or bigger than the original one. If we have, for example, a scale drawing of 1:10, this means that the drawn object is 10 times smaller than the original one. Naturally, the bigger y is, the smaller the drawn object is. However, if we have a case of 10:1, this means that the drawn object is 10 times bigger than the original one.

If we are given sizes of a drawn and an original object, we can find the scale drawing (SD) if we divide drawn size (DS) by the actual size (AS):

SD = DS/AS

If we look at the smiley faces above, and we say that the left smiley is the original image and the right is the drawn one, then the scale drawing would be 1:2, where drawn smiley is 2 times smaller than the original one. If we say that the right smiley is the original smiley, here we would have a scale drawing of 2:1, where the drawn smiley is 2 times bigger than the original one.

Example Problem:

On a map that has a scale drawing of 1:250,000, the distance between 2 cities is 2 centimeters.

What is:
- a. the actual distance
- b. distance on a map that has a scale drawing of 1:80,000?

a. We have the scale drawing and we can use x and y to make an equation: 1:250,000 = x : y

We are given the distance on map, that is the drawn size, so we put 2 centimeters instead x: 1:250,000 = 2 cm : y

Now we multiply the outside numbers, which is equal to the multiplication of the inside numbers:

1 : 250,000 = 2 cm : y

1 • y = 250,000 • 2 cm
y = 500,000 cm
y = 5,000 m
y = 5 km

b. Now that we have the actual distance, we can use it to find the drawn distance on a map with scale 1:80,000. Now we put 5 kilometers instead of y:

1 : 80,000 = x : 5 km

5 km = 80,000x   / we convert km into cm

500,000 cm = 80,000x
x = 500,000 cm : 80,000
x = 4 cm

QUADRILATERALS

Quadrilaterals are 2-dimentional geometrical shapes that have 4 sides and 4 angles. There are many types of quadrilaterals, depending on the length of its sides and if they are parallel and also depending on the size of its angles. All quadrilaterals have the following properties:

Sum of all interior angles is 360°

Sum of all exterior angles is 360°

A quadrilateral is a parallelogram is it fulfills at least one of the following conditions:

Angles on each side are supplementary
Opposite angles are equal
Opposite sides are equal
Diagonals intersect each other exactly in half

Here are some of the quadrilaterals:

Square

All sides are equal
All angles are right angles

Rectangle

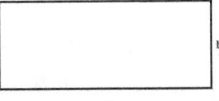

2 pairs of equal sides
All angles are right angles

Parallelogram

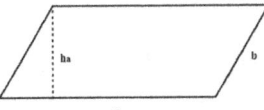

2 pairs of equal sides
Opposite angles are equal

Rhombus

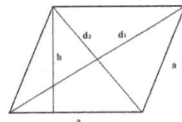

All sides are equal
Opposite angles are equal

Trapezoid

One pair of parallel sides

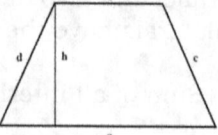

Example Problem
Find all angles of a parallelogram if one angle is greater than the other one by $40°$.

First, we draw an image of a parallelogram:

We denote angles by α and β, Since this is a parallelogram, the opposite angles are equal.

We are given that one angle is greater than the other one by $40°$, so we can write:

β = α + $40°$

We solve this problem in two ways:
1) The sum of all internal angles of every quadrilateral is $360°$. There are 2 α and 2 β. So we have:
2α + 2β = $360°$

Now, instead of β we write α + 40:
2 α + 2 (α + $40°$) = $360°$
2 α + 2 α + $80°$ = $360°$
4 α = $360°$ - $80°$
4 α = $280°$
α = $280°$ / 4
α = $70°$
Now we can find β from α:
β = α + $40°$
β = $70°$ + $40°$
β = $110°$

2) One of the conditions for parallelogram is " Angles on each

side are supplementary" and we can use that to find these angles:
$α + β = 180°$
$α + α + 40° = 180°$
$2α = 180° - 40°$
$2α = 140°$
$α = 70°$

Now we find $β$:
$β = α + 40°$
$β = 70° + 40°$
$β = 110°$

PRACTICE TEST QUESTIONS SET 1

The questions below are not the same as you will find on the CHSPE - that would be too easy! And nobody knows what the questions will be and they change all the time. Below are general questions that cover the same subject areas as the CHSPE. So, while the format and exact wording of the questions may differ slightly, and change from year to year, if you can answer the questions below, you will have no problem with the CHSPE.

For the best results, take these Practice Test Questions as if it were the real exam. Set aside time when you will not be disturbed, and a location that is quiet and free of distractions. Read the instructions carefully, read each question carefully, and answer to the best of your ability.
Use the bubbles provided. When you have completed the Practice Questions, check your answer against the Answer Key and read the explanation provided.

Do not attempt more than one set of practice test questions in one day. After completing the first practice test, wait two or three days before attempting the second set of questions.

Reading

	A	B	C	D	E		A	B	C	D	E
1	○	○	○	○	○	26	○	○	○	○	○
2	○	○	○	○	○	27	○	○	○	○	○
3	○	○	○	○	○	28	○	○	○	○	○
4	○	○	○	○	○	29	○	○	○	○	○
5	○	○	○	○	○	30	○	○	○	○	○
6	○	○	○	○	○	31	○	○	○	○	○
7	○	○	○	○	○	32	○	○	○	○	○
8	○	○	○	○	○	33	○	○	○	○	○
9	○	○	○	○	○	34	○	○	○	○	○
10	○	○	○	○	○	35	○	○	○	○	○
11	○	○	○	○	○	36	○	○	○	○	○
12	○	○	○	○	○	37	○	○	○	○	○
13	○	○	○	○	○	38	○	○	○	○	○
14	○	○	○	○	○	39	○	○	○	○	○
15	○	○	○	○	○	40	○	○	○	○	○
16	○	○	○	○	○	41	○	○	○	○	○
17	○	○	○	○	○	42	○	○	○	○	○
18	○	○	○	○	○	43	○	○	○	○	○
19	○	○	○	○	○	44	○	○	○	○	○
20	○	○	○	○	○	45	○	○	○	○	○
21	○	○	○	○	○	46	○	○	○	○	○
22	○	○	○	○	○	47	○	○	○	○	○
23	○	○	○	○	○	48	○	○	○	○	○
24	○	○	○	○	○	49	○	○	○	○	○
25	○	○	○	○	○	50	○	○	○	○	○

Language Arts

	A	B	C	D	E			A	B	C	D	E
1	○	○	○	○	○		26	○	○	○	○	○
2	○	○	○	○	○		27	○	○	○	○	○
3	○	○	○	○	○		28	○	○	○	○	○
4	○	○	○	○	○		29	○	○	○	○	○
5	○	○	○	○	○		30	○	○	○	○	○
6	○	○	○	○	○		31	○	○	○	○	○
7	○	○	○	○	○		32	○	○	○	○	○
8	○	○	○	○	○		33	○	○	○	○	○
9	○	○	○	○	○		34	○	○	○	○	○
10	○	○	○	○	○		35	○	○	○	○	○
11	○	○	○	○	○		36	○	○	○	○	○
12	○	○	○	○	○		37	○	○	○	○	○
13	○	○	○	○	○		38	○	○	○	○	○
14	○	○	○	○	○		39	○	○	○	○	○
15	○	○	○	○	○		40	○	○	○	○	○
16	○	○	○	○	○		41	○	○	○	○	○
17	○	○	○	○	○		42	○	○	○	○	○
18	○	○	○	○	○		43	○	○	○	○	○
19	○	○	○	○	○		44	○	○	○	○	○
20	○	○	○	○	○		45	○	○	○	○	○
21	○	○	○	○	○		46	○	○	○	○	○
22	○	○	○	○	○		47	○	○	○	○	○
23	○	○	○	○	○		48	○	○	○	○	○
24	○	○	○	○	○		49	○	○	○	○	○
25	○	○	○	○	○		50	○	○	○	○	○

Mathematics

	A	B	C	D	E		A	B	C	D	E
1	○	○	○	○	○	26	○	○	○	○	○
2	○	○	○	○	○	27	○	○	○	○	○
3	○	○	○	○	○	28	○	○	○	○	○
4	○	○	○	○	○	29	○	○	○	○	○
5	○	○	○	○	○	30	○	○	○	○	○
6	○	○	○	○	○	31	○	○	○	○	○
7	○	○	○	○	○	32	○	○	○	○	○
8	○	○	○	○	○	33	○	○	○	○	○
9	○	○	○	○	○	34	○	○	○	○	○
10	○	○	○	○	○	35	○	○	○	○	○
11	○	○	○	○	○	36	○	○	○	○	○
12	○	○	○	○	○	37	○	○	○	○	○
13	○	○	○	○	○	38	○	○	○	○	○
14	○	○	○	○	○	39	○	○	○	○	○
15	○	○	○	○	○	40	○	○	○	○	○
16	○	○	○	○	○	41	○	○	○	○	○
17	○	○	○	○	○	42	○	○	○	○	○
18	○	○	○	○	○	43	○	○	○	○	○
19	○	○	○	○	○	44	○	○	○	○	○
20	○	○	○	○	○	45	○	○	○	○	○
21	○	○	○	○	○	46	○	○	○	○	○
22	○	○	○	○	○	47	○	○	○	○	○
23	○	○	○	○	○	48	○	○	○	○	○
24	○	○	○	○	○	49	○	○	○	○	○
25	○	○	○	○	○	50	○	○	○	○	○

READING AND LANGUAGE ARTS

Directions: The following questions are based on several reading passages. A series of questions follow each passage. Read each passage carefully, and then answer the questions based on it. You may reread the passage as often as you wish. When you have finished answering the questions based on one passage, go right onto the next passage. Choose the best answer based on the information given and implied.

Questions 1 – 4 refer to the following passage.

Passage 1 - The Life of Helen Keller

Many people have heard of Helen Keller. She is famous because she was unable to see or hear, but learned to speak and read and went onto attend college and earn a degree. Her life is a very interesting story, one that she developed into an autobiography, which was then adapted into both a stage play and a movie. How did Helen Keller overcome her disabilities to become a famous woman? Read on to find out. Helen Keller was not born blind and deaf. When she was a small baby, she had a very high fever for several days. As a result of her sudden illness, baby Helen lost her eyesight and her hearing. Because she was so young when she went deaf and blind, Helen Keller never had any recollection of being able to see or hear. Since she could not hear, she could not learn to talk. Since she could not see, it was difficult for her to move around. For the first six years of her life, her world was very still and dark.

Imagine what Helen's childhood was like. She could not hear her mother's voice. She could not see the beauty of her parent's farm. She could not recognize who was giving her a hug, or a bath or even where her bedroom was each night. Worse, she could not communicate with her parents in any way. She could not express her feelings or tell them the things she wanted. It must have been a very sad childhood.

When Helen was six years old, her parents hired her a teacher named Anne Sullivan. Anne was a young woman who was almost blind. However, she could hear and she could read Braille, so she was a perfect teacher for young Helen. At first, Anne had a very hard time teaching Helen anything. She described her first impression of Helen as a "wild thing, not a child." Helen did not like Anne at first either. She bit and hit Anne when Anne tried to teach her. However, the two of them eventually came to have a great deal of love and respect.

Anne taught Helen to hear by putting her hands on people's throats. She could feel the sounds people made. In time, Helen learned to feel what people said. Next, Anne taught Helen to read Braille, which is a way that books are written for the blind. Finally, Anne taught Helen to talk. Although Helen did learn to talk, it was hard for anyone but Anne to understand her.

As Helen grew older, she amazed more and more people with her story. She went to college and wrote books about her life. She gave talks to the public, with Anne at her side, translating her words. Today, both Anne Sullivan and Helen Keller are famous women who are respected for their lives' work.

1. Helen Keller could not see and hear and so, what was her biggest problem in childhood?

    a. Inability to communicate

    b. Inability to walk

    c. Inability to play

    d. Inability to eat

2. Helen learned to hear by feeling the vibrations people made when they spoke. What were these vibrations were felt through?

    a. Mouth

    b. Throat

    c. Ears

    d. Lips

3. From the passage, we can infer that Anne Sullivan was a patient teacher. We can infer this because

    a. Helen hit and bit her and Anne remained her teacher.

    b. Anne taught Helen to read only.

    c. Anne was hard of hearing too.

    d. Anne wanted to be a teacher.

4. Helen Keller learned to speak but Anne translated her words when she spoke in public. The reason Helen needed a translator was because

    a. Helen spoke another language.

    b. Helen's words were hard for people to understand.

    c. Helen spoke very quietly.

    d. Helen did not speak but only used sign language.

Questions 5 – 7 refer to the following passage.

Passage 2 - Ways Characters Communicate in Theater

Playwrights give their characters voices in a way that gives depth and added meaning to what happens on stage during their play. There are different types of speech in scripts that allow characters to talk with themselves, with other characters, and even with the audience.

It is very unique to theater that characters may talk "to themselves." When characters do this, the speech they give is called a soliloquy. Soliloquies are usually poetic, introspective, moving, and can tell audience members about the feelings, motivations, or suspicions of an individual character without that character having to reveal them to other characters on stage. "To be or not to be" is a famous soliloquy given by Hamlet as he considers difficult but important themes, such as life and death.

The most common type of communication in plays is when one character is speaking to another or a group of other characters. This is generally called dialogue, but can also be called monologue if one character speaks without being interrupted for a long time. It is not necessarily the most important type of communication, but it is the most common because the plot of the play cannot really progress without it.

Lastly, and most unique to theater (although it has been used somewhat in film) is when a character speaks directly to the audience. This is called an aside, and scripts usually specifically direct actors to do this. Asides are usually comical, an inside joke between the character and the audience, and very short. The actor will usually face the audience when delivering them, even if it's for a moment, so the audience can recognize this move as an aside.

All three of these types of communication are important to the art of theater, and have been perfected by famous playwrights like Shakespeare. Understanding these types of communication can help an audience member grasp what is artful about the script and action of a play.

5. According to the passage, characters in plays communicate to

    a. move the plot forward

    b. show the private thoughts and feelings of one character

    c. make the audience laugh

    d. add beauty and artistry to the play

6. When Hamlet delivers "To be or not to be," he can most likely be described as

    a. solitary

    b. thoughtful

    c. dramatic

    d. hopeless

7. The author uses parentheses to punctuate "although it has been used somewhat in film,"

    a. to show that films are less important

    b. instead of using commas so that the sentence is not interrupted

    c. because parenthesis help separate details that are not as important

    d. to show that films are not as artistic

Questions 8 – 11 refer to the following passage.

Passage 3 - Low Blood Sugar

As the name suggest, low blood sugar is low sugar levels in the bloodstream. This can occur when you have not eaten properly and undertake strenuous activity, or, when you are very hungry. When Low blood sugar occurs regularly and is ongoing, it is a medical condition called hypoglycemia. This condition can occur in diabetics and in healthy adults.

Causes of low blood sugar can include excessive alcohol consumption, metabolic problems, stomach surgery, pancreas, liver or kidneys problems, as well as a side-effect of some medications.

Symptoms

There are different symptoms depending on the severity of the case.

Mild hypoglycemia can lead to feelings of nausea and hunger. The patient may also feel nervous, jittery and have fast heart beats. Sweaty skin, clammy and cold skin are likely symptoms.
Moderate hypoglycemia can result in a short temper, confusion, nervousness, fear and blurring of vision. The patient may feel weak and unsteady.

Severe cases of hypoglycemia can lead to seizures, coma,

fainting spells, nightmares, headaches, excessive sweats and severe tiredness.

Diagnosis of low blood sugar

A doctor can diagnosis this medical condition by asking the patient questions and testing blood and urine samples. Home testing kits are available for patients to monitor blood sugar levels. It is important to see a qualified doctor though. A doctor can administer tests to safely rule out other medical conditions that could affect blood sugar levels.

Treatment

Quick treatments include drinking or eating foods and drinks with high sugar contents. Good examples include soda, fruit juice, hard candy and raisins. Glucose energy tablets can also help. Doctors may also recommend medications and well as changes in diet and exercise routine to treat chronic low blood sugar.

8. Based on the article, which of the following is true?

    a. Low blood sugar can happen to anyone.

    b. Low blood sugar only happens to diabetics.

    c. Low blood sugar can occur even.

    d. None of the statements are true.

9. Which of the following are the author's opinion?

    a. Quick treatments include drinking or eating foods and drinks with high sugar contents.

    b. None of the statements are opinions.

    c. This condition can occur in diabetics and also in healthy adults.

    d. There are different symptoms depending on the severity of the case

10. What is the author's purpose?

    a. To inform

    b. To persuade

    c. To entertain

    d. To analyze

11. Which of the following is not a detail?

    a. A doctor can diagnosis this medical condition by asking the patient questions and testing.

    b. A doctor will test blood and urine samples.

    c. Glucose energy tablets can also help.

    d. Home test kits monitor blood sugar levels.

    d. None of the above.

Questions 12 – 15 refer to the following passage.

How To Get A Good Nights Sleep

Sleep is just as essential for healthy living as water, air and food. Sleep allows the body to rest and replenish depleted energy levels. Sometimes we may, for various reasons, have trouble sleeping which has a serious effect on our health. Those who have prolonged sleeping problems are facing a serious medical condition and should see a qualified doctor when possible for help. Here is simple guide that can help you sleep better at night.

Try to create a natural pattern of waking up and sleeping around the same time every day. This means avoiding going to bed too early and oversleeping past your usual wake up time. Going to bed and getting up at radically different times everyday confuses your body clock. Try to establish a natural rhythm as much as you can.

Exercises and a bit of physical activity can help you sleep better at night. If you are having problem sleeping, try to be as active as you can during the day. If you are tired from physical activity, falling asleep is a natural and easy process for your body. If you remain inactive during the day, you will find it harder to sleep properly at night. Try walking, jogging, swimming or simple stretches as you get close to your bed time.

Afternoon naps are great to refresh you during the day, but they may also keep you awake at night. If you feel sleepy during the day, get up, take a walk and get busy to keep from sleeping. Stretching is a good way to increase blood flow to the brain and keep you alert so that you don't sleep during the day. This will help you sleep better night.

> A warm bath or a glass of milk in the evening can help your body relax and prepare for sleep. A cold bath will wake you up and keep you up for several hours. Also avoid eating too late before bed.

12. How would you describe this sentence?

    a. A recommendation

    b. An opinion

    c. A fact

    d. A diagnosis

13. Which of the following is an alternative title for this article?

    a. Exercise and a good night's sleep

    b. Benefits of a good night's sleep

    c. Tips for a good night's sleep

    d. Lack of sleep is a serious medical condition

14. Which of the following cannot be inferred from this article?

    a. Biking is helpful for getting a good night's sleep

    b. Mental activity is helpful for getting a good night's sleep

    c. Eating bedtime snacks is not recommended

    d. Getting up at the same time is helpful for a good night's sleep

15. What is a disadvantage of taking naps?

    a. They may keep you awake.

    b. There are no disadvantages

    c. They may help you sleep better

    d. They may affect your diet

Question 16 refers to the following Table of Contents.

Contents

    Science Self-assessment 81
    Answer Key 91
    Science Tutorials 96
    Scientific Method 96
    Biology 99
    Heredity: Genes and Mutation 104
    Classification 108
    Ecology 110
    Chemistry 112
    Energy: Kinetic and Mechanical 126
    Energy: Work and Power 130
    Force: Newton's Three Laws 132

16. Consider the table of contents above. What page would you find information about natural selection and adaptation?

    a. 81
    b. 90
    c. 110
    d. 132

Questions 17 – 20 refer to the following passage.

Passage 5 - Pearl Harbor

A Day That Will Live in Infamy! Attack on Pearl Harbor
In 1941, the world was at war. The United States was trying very hard to keep itself out of the conflict. In Europe, the countries of Germany and Italy had formed an alliance to expand their land and territory. Germany had already taken over Poland, Denmark, and parts of France. They were heading next toward England and due to all the fighting in Europe, there were battles taking place as far south as North Africa, where the German and Italian armies were fighting the British.

This got even worse when the Asian nation of Japan formed an alliance with Germany and Italy. Together, the three countries called themselves, the AXIS. Now, the war was in the Pacific as well as in Europe and Northern Africa. A great deal of Americans felt that perhaps now was the time for the United States to join with its ally, Great Britain and stop the Axis from taking over more regions of the world.

In 1941, Franklin Roosevelt was President of the United States. His fear at the time was that Japan would try to take over many countries in Asia. He did not want to see that happen, so he moved some of the United States warships that had been stationed in San Diego, to the military base at Pearl Harbor, in Honolulu, Hawaii.

Japan quietly plotted their attack. They waited until the

early hours of the morning on Sunday, December 7, 1941. Then, 350 Japanese war plans began to drop bombs on the U.S. ships at Pearl Harbor. The first bombs fell at 7:48 am and a mere 90 minutes later, the attack was over. Pearl Harbor was decimated. 8 battleships were damaged. Eleven ships were sunk and 300 U.S. planes were destroyed. Most devastating was the loss of life 2,400 U.S. military members was killed in the attack and 1,282 were injured.

President Roosevelt addressed the country via the radio and said "Today is a day that will live in infamy." He asked Congress to declare war on Japan. War was declared on Japan on December 8th and on Germany and Italy on December 11th. The United States had entered World War Two.

17. After reading the passage, what can we infer infamy means?

    a. Famous

    b. Remembered in a good way

    c. Remembered in a bad way

    d. Easily forgotten

18. What three countries formed the Axis?

    a. Italy, England, Germany

    b. United States, England, Italy

    c. Germany, Japan, Italy

    d. Germany, Japan, United States

19. What do you think was President Roosevelt's reason for moving warships to Pearl Harbor?

    a. He feared Japan would bomb San Diego

    b. He knew Japan was going to attack Pearl Harbor

    c. He was planning to attack Japan

    d. He wanted to try and protect Asian countries from Japanese takeover

20. Why do you think Japan chose a Sunday morning at 7:48 am for their attack?

   a. They knew the military slept late

   b. There is a law against bombing countries on a Sunday

   c. They wanted the attack to catch people by surprise

   d. That was the only free time they had to attack.

Questions 21 - 24 refer to the following recipe.

If You Have Allergies, You're Not Alone

People who experience allergies might joke that their immune systems have let them down or are seriously lacking. Truthfully though, people who experience allergic reactions or allergy symptoms during certain times of the year have heightened immune systems that are, "better" than those of people who have perfectly healthy but less militant immune systems.

Still, when a person has an allergic reaction, they are having an adverse reaction to a substance that is considered normal to most people. Mild allergic reactions usually have symptoms like itching, runny nose, red eyes, or bumps or discoloration of the skin. More serious allergic reactions, such as those to animal and insect poisons or certain foods, may result in the closing of the throat, swelling of the eyes, low blood pressure, inability to breath, and can even be fatal.

Different treatments help different allergies, and which one a person uses depends on the nature and severity of the allergy. It is recommended to patients with severe allergies to take extra precautions, such as carrying an EpiPen, which treats anaphylactic shock and may prevent death, always in order for the remedy to be readily available and more effective. When an allergy is not so severe, treatments may be used just relieve a person of uncomfortable symptoms. Over the counter allergy medicines treat milder symptoms, and can be bought at any grocery store and used in moderation to help people with allergies live normally.

There are many tests available to assess whether a person

has allergies or what they may be allergic to, and advances in these tests and the medicine used to treat patients continues to improve. Despite this fact, allergies still affect many people throughout the year or even every day. Medicines used to treat allergies have side effects of their own, and it is difficult to bring the body into balance with the use of medicine. Regardless, many of those who live with allergies are grateful for what is available and find it useful in maintaining their lifestyles.

21. According to this passage, the word that the word "militant" belongs in a group with the words:

    a. sickly, ailing, faint

    b. strength, power, vigor

    c. active, fighting, warring

    d. worn, tired, breaking down

22. The author says that "medicines used to treat allergies have side-effects of their own" to

    a. point out that doctors aren't very good at diagnosing and treating allergies

    b. argue that because of the large number of people with allergies, a cure will never be found

    c. explain that allergy medicines aren't cures and some compromise must be made

    d. argue that more wholesome remedies should be researched and medicines banned

23. It can be inferred that _____ recommend that some people with allergies carry medicine with them.

    a. the author

    b. doctors

    c. the makers of EpiPen

    d. people with allergies

24. The author has written this passage to

    a. inform readers on symptoms of allergies so people with allergies can get help

    b. persuade readers to be proud of having allergies

    c. inform readers on different remedies so people with allergies receive the right help

    d. describe different types of allergies, their symptoms, and their remedies

Questions 25 – 26 refer to the following email.

SUBJECT: MEDICAL STAFF CHANGES

To all staff:

This email is to advise you of a paper on recommended medical staff changes has been posted to the Human Resources website.

The contents are of primary interest to medical staff, other staff may be interested in reading it, particularly those in medical support roles.

The paper deals with several major issues:

    1. Improving our ability to attract top quality staff to the hospital, and retain our existing staff. These changes will make our position and departmental names internationally recognizable and comparable with North American and North Asian departments and positions.

    2. Improving our ability to attract top quality staff by introducing greater flexibility in the departmental structure.

    3. General comments on issues to be further discussed in relation to research staff.

The changes outlined in this paper are significant. I encourage you to read the document and send to me any comments you may have, so that it can be enhanced and improved.

Gordon Simms
Administrator,
Seven Oaks Regional Hospital

**25. Are all hospital staff required to read the document posted to the
Human Resources website?**

    a. Yes all staff are required to read the document.

    b. No, reading the document is optional.

    c. Only medical staff are required to read the document.

    d. none of the above are correct.

26. Have the changes to medical staff been made?

    a. Yes, the changes have been made.

    b. No, the changes are only being discussed.

    c. Some of the changes have been made.

    d. None of the choices are correct.

Questions 27 – 30 refer to the following passage.

When a Poet Longs to Mourn, He Writes an Elegy

Poems are an expressive, especially emotional, form of writing. They have been present in literature virtually from the time civilizations invented the written word. Poets often portrayed as moody, secluded, and even troubled, but this is because poets are introspective and feel deeply about the current events and cultural norms they are surrounded with. Poets often produce the most telling literature, giving insight into the society and mind-set they come from. This can be done in many forms.

The oldest types of poems often include many stanzas, may

or may not rhyme, and are more about telling a story than experimenting with language or words. The most common types of ancient poetry are epics, which are usually extremely long stories that follow a hero through his journey, or ellegies, which are often solemn in tone and used to mourn or lament something or someone. The Mesopotamians are often said to have invented the written word, and their literature is among the oldest in the world, including the epic poem titled "Epic of Gilgamesh." Similar in style and length to "Gilgamesh" is "Beowulf," an ellegy written in Old English and set in Scandinavia. These poems are often used by professors as the earliest examples of literature.

The importance of poetry was revived in the Renaissance. At this time, Europeans discovered the style and beauty of ancient Greek arts, and poetry was among those. Shakespeare is the most well-known poet of the time, and he used poetry not only to write poems but also to write plays for the theater. The most popular forms of poetry during the Renaissance included villanelles, (a nineteen-line poetic form) sonnets, as well as the epic. Poets during this time focused on style and form, and developed very specific rules and outlines for how an exceptional poem should be written.

As often happens in the arts, modern poets have rejected the constricting rules of Renaissance poets, and free form poems are much more popular. Some modern poems would read just like stories if they weren't arranged into lines and stanzas. It is difficult to tell which poems and poets will be the most important, because works of art often become more famous in hindsight, after the poet has died and society can look at itself without being in the moment. Modern poetry continues to develop, and will no doubt continue to change as values, thought, and writing continue to change.

Poems can be among the most enlightening and uplifting texts for a person to read if they are looking to connect with the past, connect with other people, or try to gain an understanding of what is happening in their time.

27. In summary, the author has written this passage

a. as a foreword that will introduce a poem in a book or magazine

b. because she loves poetry and wants more people to like it

c. to give a brief history of poems

d. to convince students to write poems

28. The author organizes the paragraphs mainly by

a. moving chronologically, explaining which types of poetry were common in that time

b. talking about new types of poems each paragraph and explaining them a little

c. focusing on one poet or group of people and the poems they wrote

d. explaining older types of poetry so she can talk about modern poetry

29. The author's claim that poetry has been around "virtually from the time civilizations invented the written word" is supported by the detail that

a. Beowulf is written in Old English, which is not really in use any longer

b. epic poems told stories about heroes

c. the Renaissance poets tried to copy Greek poets

d. the Mesopotamians are credited with both inventing the word and writing "Epic of Gilgamesh"

30. According to the passage, the word that the word "telling" means

a. speaking

b. significant

c. soothing

d. wordy

31. Choose a verb that means fearless or invulnerable to intimidation and fear.

    a. Feeble
    b. Strongest
    c. Dauntless
    d. Super

32. Choose a word that means the same as the underlined word.

I see the differences when they are placed side-by-side and juxtaposed.

    a. Compared
    b. Eliminated
    c. Overturned
    d. Exonerated

33. Choose the meaning of regicide.

    a. v. To endow or furnish with requisite ability, character, knowledge and skill
    b. n. killing of a king
    c. adj. Disposed to seize by violence or by unlawful or greedy methods
    d. v. To refresh after labor

34. Choose the best definition of pernicious.

    a. Deadly
    b. Infectious
    c. Common
    d. Rare

35. After she received her influenza vaccination, Nan thought that she was _____ to the common cold.

    a. Immune
    b. Susceptible
    c. Vulnerable
    d. At risk

36. She performed the gymnastics and stretches so well! I have never seen anyone so <u>nimble</u>.

    a. Awkward
    b. Agile
    c. Quick
    d. Taut

37. Are there any more <u>queries</u>? We have already had so many questions today.

    a. Questions
    b. Commands
    c. Obfuscations
    d. Paradoxes

38. Choose a verb that means to remove a leader or high official from position.

    a. Sack
    b. Suspend
    c. Depose
    d. Dropped

39. Choose the best definition of pedestrian.

    a. Rare
    b. Often
    c. Walking or Running
    d. Commonplace

40. Choose the best definition of petulant.

   a. Patient
   b. Childish
   c. Impatient
   d. Mature

41. Paul's rose bushes were being destroyed by Japanese beetles, so he invested in a good _____ .

   a. Fungicide
   b. Fertilizer
   c. Sprinkler
   d. Pesticide

42. Choose the best definition of salient.

   a. v. To make light by fermentation, as dough
   b. adj. Not stringent or energetic
   c. adj. negligible
   d. adj. worthy of note or relevant

43. Choose the best definition of sedentary

   a. n. A morbid condition, due to obstructed excretion of bile or characterized by yellowing of the skin
   b. adj. not moving or sitting at a place
   c. v. To wander from place to place
   d. n. Perplexity

44. The last time that the crops failed, the entire nation experienced months of _____ .

   a. Famine
   b. Harvest
   c. Plenitude
   d. Disease

45. Choose the best definition of stint.

    a. Thrifty
    b. Annoyed
    c. Dislike
    d. Insult

46. Choose the best definition of precipitate.

    a. To rain
    b. To throw down
    c. To throw up
    d. to snow

47. Choose the verb that means to build up or strengthen in relation to morals or religion.

    a. Sanctify
    b. Amplify
    c. Edify
    d. Wry

48. Choose the noun that means exit or way out.

    a. Door-jamb
    b. Egress
    c. Regress
    d. Furtherance

49. Choose the best definition of the underlined word.

The tide was in this morning but now it is starting to <u>recede</u>.

    a. Go out
    b. Flow
    c. Swell
    d. Come in

50. Choose the word that means private, personal.

    a. Confidential
    b. Hysteric
    c. Simplistic
    d. Promissory

English Grammar, Punctuation, Capitalization and Usage

Directions: Carefully examine the underlined words in the sentences given below. You may see an error in punctuation, grammar, usage or capitalization. Select the correct version of the sentence from the choices given.

1. To make chicken <u>soup; you</u> must first buy a chicken.

    a. To make chicken soup you must first buy a chicken.
    b. To make chicken soup you must first, buy a chicken.
    c. To make chicken soup, you must first buy a chicken.
    d. None of the choices are correct.

2. To travel around <u>the globe you have</u> to drive 25,000 miles.

    a. To travel around the globe, you have to drive 25000 miles.

    b. To travel around the globe, you have to drive, 25000 miles.

    c. None of the choices are correct.

    d. To travel around the globe, you have to drive 25,000 miles.

3. The dog loved chasing <u>bones; but never ate them:</u> it was running that he enjoyed.

    a. The dog loved chasing bones, but never ate them; it was running that he enjoyed.

    b. The dog loved chasing bones; but never ate them, it was running that he enjoyed.

    c. The dog loved chasing bones, but never ate them, it was running that he enjoyed.

    d. None of the choices are correct.

4. He had not paid the <u>rent, therefore,</u> the landlord changed the locks.

    a. None of the choices are correct.

    b. He had not paid the rent; therefore, the landlord changed the locks.

    c. He had not paid the rent, therefore; the landlord changed the locks.

    d. He had not paid the rent therefore, the landlord changed the locks.

5. If **he would have known** about the forecast, he would **have postponed** the camping trip.

a. He would have postponed the camping trip, if he would have known about the forecast.

b. None of the choices are correct.

c. If he have known about the forecast, he would have postponed the camping trip.

d. If he had known about the forecast, he would have postponed the camping trip.

6. Although you may not see **nobody** in the dark, it does not mean that **nobody** is there.

a. The sentence is correct.

b. Although you may not see anyone in the dark, it does not mean that not nobody is there.

c. Although you may not see anyone in the dark, it does not mean that anyone is there.

d. Although you may not see nobody in the dark, it does not mean that not nobody is there.

7. He **don't** have any money to buy clothes and neither **does** I.

a. He doesn't have any money to buy clothes and neither do I.

b. He doesn't have any money to buy clothes and neither does I.

c. He don't have any money to buy clothes and neither do I.

d. None of the choices are correct.

8. Choose the sentence with the correct grammar.

    a. Because it really don't matter, I don't care if I go there.
    b. Because it really doesn't matter, I doesn't care if I go there.
    c. Because it really doesn't matter, I don't care if I go there.
    d. Because it really don't matter, I don't care if I go there.

9. When we <u>go</u> to the picnic, we will <u>take</u> potato salad and wieners.

    a. None of the choices are correct.

    b. If you come to the picnic, bring potato salad and wieners.

    c. When we go to the picnic, we will bring potato salad and wieners.

    d. If you come to the picnic, take potato salad and wieners.

10. The older children <u>have already eat</u> their dinner, but the baby has <u>not yet ate</u> anything.

    a. The older children have already eat their dinner, but the baby has not yet eaten anything.

    b. The older children have already eaten their dinner, but the baby has not yet ate anything.

    c. The older children have already eaten their dinner, but the baby has not yet eaten anything.

    d. The sentence is correct.

11. Newer cars use <u>less</u> gasoline, and produce <u>less</u> emissions.

a. Newer cars use fewer gasoline, and produce fewer emissions.

b. None of the choices are correct.

c. Newer cars use less gasoline, and produce fewer emissions.

d. Newer cars fewer less gasoline, and produce less emissions.

12. He should have <u>went</u> to the appointment; instead, he <u>gone</u> to the beach.

a. He should have went to the appointment; instead, he went to the beach.

b. He should have gone to the appointment; instead, he went to the beach.

c. None of the choices are correct.

d. He should have gone to the appointment; instead, he gone to the beach.

13. <u>However;</u> I believe that he didn't really try that hard.

a. However, I believe that he didn't really try that hard.

b. However I believe that he didn't really try that hard.

c. None of the choices are correct.

d. However: I believe that he didn't really try that hard.

14. It's important for you to know <u>it's</u> official name; <u>it's</u> called the Confederate Museum.

a. Its important for you to know its official name; its called the Confederate Museum.

b. None of the choices are correct.

c. It's important for you to know its official name; it's called the Confederate Museum.

d. Its important for you to know it's official name; it's called the Confederate Museum.

15. Once the chickens had laid their eggs, they laid on their nests to hatch them.

    a. Once the chickens had layed their eggs, they lay on their nests to hatch them.

    b. Once the chickens had lay their eggs, they lay on their nests to hatch them.

    c. Once the chickens had laid their eggs, they lay on their nests to hatch them.

    d. None of the choices are correct.

16. The mother <u>would not of punished</u> her daughter if she <u>could of avoided</u> it.

    a. The mother would not of punished her daughter if she could have avoided it.

    b. The mother would not have punished her daughter if she could of avoided it.

    c. None of the choices are correct.

    d. The mother would not have punished her daughter if she could have avoided it.

17. Even with <u>an</u> speed limit sign clearly posted, <u>a</u> inattentive driver may drive too fast.

    a. Even with an speed limit sign clearly posted, an inattentive driver may drive too fast.

    b. Even with a speed limit sign clearly posted, a inattentive driver may drive too fast.

    c. None of the choices are correct.

    d. Even with a speed limit sign clearly posted, an inattentive driver may drive too fast.

18. **Accept for the roses, she did not accept John's frequent gifts.**

   a. Except for the roses, she did not accept John's frequent gifts.
   b. Accept for the roses, she did not except John's frequent gifts.
   c. None of the choices are correct.
   d. Except for the roses, she did not except John's frequent gifts.

19. **Although he continued to advice me, I no longer took his advise.**

   a. Although he continued to advise me, I no longer took his advice.
   b. Although he continued to advice me, I no longer took his advise.
   c. Although he continued to advise me, I no longer took his advise.
   d. None of the choices are correct.

20. **To adopt to the climate, we had to adopt a different style of clothing.**

   a. To adapt to the climate, we had to adapt a different style of clothing.
   b. To adopt to the climate, we had to adopt a different style of clothing.
   c. To adapt to the climate, we had to adopt a different style of clothing.
   d. None of the choices are correct.

21. **When he's <u>between</u> friends, Robert seems confident, but, <u>between</u> you and me, he is really shy.**

   a. None of the choices are correct.

   b. When he's among friends, Robert seems confident, but, among you and me, he is really shy.

   c. When he's between friends, Robert seems confident, but, among you and me, he is really shy.

   d. When he's among friends, Robert seems confident, but, between you and me, he is really shy.

22. **I will be finished <u>at about</u> ten in the morning, and will be arriving at home <u>at</u> 6:30.**

   a. I will be finished at ten in the morning, and will be arriving at home at about 6:30.

   b. None of the choices are correct.

   c. I will be finished at about ten in the morning, and will be arriving at home at about 6:30.

   d. I will be finished at ten in the morning, and will be arriving at home at 6:30.

23. **<u>Beside</u> the red curtains and pillows, there was a red rug <u>besides</u> the couch.**

   a. Beside the red curtains and pillows, there was a red rug beside the couch.

   b. Besides the red curtains and pillows, there was a red rug beside the couch.

   c. Besides the red curtains and pillows, there was a red rug besides the couch.

   d. None of the choices are correct.

24. Although John <u>may</u> swim very well, the lifeguard <u>may</u> not allow him to swim in the pool.

    a. Although John can swim very well, the lifeguard may not allow him to swim in the pool.

    b. None of the choices are correct.

    c. Although John can swim very well, the lifeguard can not allow him to swim in the pool.

    d. Although John may swim very well, the lifeguard may not allow him to swim in the pool.

25. Her <u>continuous</u> absences caused a <u>continuous</u> disruption at the office.

    a. Her continuous absences caused a continual disruption at the office.

    b. Her continual absences caused a continuous disruption at the office.

    c. Her continual absences caused a continual disruption at the office.

    d. None of the choices are correct.

26. During the famine, the Irish people had to <u>immigrate</u> to other countries; many of them <u>immigrated</u> to the United States.

    a. During the famine, the Irish people had to emigrate to other countries; many of them immigrated to the United States.

    b. None of the choices are correct.

    c. During the famine, the Irish people had to emigrate to other countries; many of them emigrated to the United States.

    d. During the famine, the Irish people had to immigrate to other countries; many of them emigrated to the United States.

27. His home was <u>further</u> than we expected; <u>further</u>, the roads were very bad.

> a. His home was farther than we expected; farther, the roads were very bad.
>
> b. His home was farther than we expected; further, the roads were very bad.
>
> c. None of the choices are correct.
>
> d. His home was further than we expected; farther, the roads were very bad.

28. The volunteers brought groceries and toys to the homeless shelter; the latter was given to the staff, while the groceries were given directly to the children.

> a. The volunteers brought groceries and toys to the homeless shelter; the latter were given to the staff, while the former were given directly to the children.
> b. The volunteers brought groceries and toys to the homeless shelter; the former was given to the staff, while the latter was given directly to the children.
> c. The volunteers brought groceries and toys to the homeless shelter; the groceries were given to the staff, while the former was given directly to the children.
> d. None of the choices are correct.

29. You shouldn't <u>sit</u> in that chair wearing black pants; I <u>sit</u> the white cat there just a moment ago.

> a. You shouldn't sit in that chair wearing black pants; I set the white cat there just a moment ago.
>
> b. You shouldn't set in that chair wearing black pants; I sit the white cat there just a moment ago.
>
> c. You shouldn't set in that chair wearing black pants; I set the white cat there just a moment ago.
>
> d. None of the choices are correct.

30. Mars is the god of war.

   a. Mars is the god or war.
   b. Mars is the God of war.
   c. Mars is the God of War.
   d. None of the choices are correct.

31. This is her third term as <u>Mayor of chicago</u>.

   a. This is her third term as mayor of Chicago.
   b. This is her third term as Mayor of Chicago.
   c. This is her third term as mayor of chicago.
   d. None of the above.

32. I was able to speak with Susan Roberts <u>mayor of tampa</u>.

   a. I was able to speak with Susan Roberts, Mayor of Tampa.
   b. I was able to speak with Susan Roberts, mayor of Tampa.
   c. I was able to speak with Susan Roberts, Mayor of tampa.
   d. None of the Above.

33. I think <u>thanksgiving</u> is the best <u>Fall Holiday</u>.

   a. I think thanksgiving is the best fall holiday.
   b. I think Thanksgiving is the best Fall holiday.
   c. I think Thanksgiving is the best fall holiday.
   d. None of the above.

34. I will be skipping The Fall 2013 semester.

   a. I will be skipping the Fall 2013 Semester.
   b. I will be skipping the fall 2013 semester.
   c. I will be skipping the Fall 2013 semester.
   d. None of the above.

35. The man was asked to come with <u>her</u> daughter and <u>his</u> test results.

    a. The man was asked to come with his daughter and her test results.

    b. The man was asked to come with her daughter and her test results.

    c. The man was asked to come with her daughter and our test results.

    d. None of the above.

36. The tables were layed by the students.

    a. The tables were laid by the students.

    b. The tables were lay by the students.

    c. The tables were lie by the students.

    d. None of the choices are correct.

37. Each boy and girl <u>were</u> given a toy.

    a. Each boy and girl were given a toy.

    b. Each boy and girl was given a toy.

    c. A and B are correct.

    d. None of the choices are correct.

38. His measles <u>are</u> getting better.

    a. His measles is getting better.

    b. The sentence is correct.

    c. Both of the choices are correct.

    d. None of the choices are correct.

39. Despite bad weather yesterday, he <u>can</u> still attend the party.

    a. The sentence is correct.

    b. Despite bad weather yesterday, he could still attend the party.

    c. Despite bad weather yesterday, he may still attend the party.

    d. None of the choices are correct.

40. Any girl that fails the test loses <u>her</u> admission.

    a. Any girl that fails the test loses their admission.

    b. Any girl that fails the test loses our admission.

    c. The sentence is correct.

    d. None of the choices are correct.

41. He <u>ought</u> be back by now.

    a. He ought to be back by now.

    b. The sentence is correct.

    c. He ought come back by now.

    d. None of the choices are correct.

42. The man as well as his son <u>have</u> arrived.

    a. The man as well as his son has arrived

    b. The sentence is correct.

    c. None of the choices are correct.

43. Mark and Peter have talked <u>to each other</u>.

    a. The sentence is correct.

    b. Mark and Peter have talked to one another.

    c. None of the choices are correct.

44. Christians believe that their lord <u>have</u> raise.

    a. Christians believe that their lord have raised.

    b. Christians believe that their lord has risen.

    c. The sentence is correct.

    d. None of the choices are correct.

45. Here are the names of people <u>whom</u> you should contact.

    a. The sentence is correct.

    b. Here are the names of people who you should contact

    c. None of the choices are correct.

46. The sad news <u>are</u> delivered this morning.

    a. The sad news were delivered this morning.

    b. The sentence is correct.

    c. The sad news was delivered this morning.

    d. None of the choices are correct.

47. The World Health Organization (WHO) <u>are</u> meeting by January.

    a. The sentence is correct.

    b. The World Health Organization (WHO) is meeting by January.

    c. None of the choices are correct.

48. They shall have to retire when they reach 60 years of age.

    a. They will have to retire when they reach 60 years of age.
    b. The sentence is correct.
    c. None of the choices are correct.

MATHEMATICS

1. Translate the following into an equation:

six times a number plus five.

    a. 6X + 5
    b. 6(X+5)
    c. 5X + 6
    d. (6 * 5) + 5

2. Translate the following into an equation:

three plus a number times 7 equals 42.

    a. 7(3 + X) = 42
    b. 3(X + 7) = 42
    c. 3X + 7 = 42
    d. (3 + 7)X = 42

3. Brad has agreed to buy everyone a Coke. Each drink costs $1.89, and there are 5 friends. Estimate Brad's cost.

    a. $7
    b. $8
    c. $10
    d. $12

4. Estimate 215 x 65.

   a. 1,350
   b. 13,500
   c. 103,500
   d. 3,500

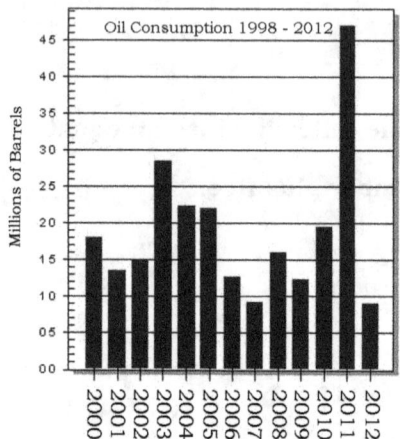

5. The graph above shows oil consumption in millions of barrels for the period, 1998 - 2012. What year did oil consumption peak?

   a. 2011
   b. 2010
   c. 2008
   d. 2009

6. In a certain game, a coin and a dice are rolled, and a player wins if the coin comes up heads, or the dice with a number greater than 4. In 20 games, about how many times will a player win?

   a. 13
   b. 8
   c. 11
   d. 15

7. Sarah weighs 25 pounds more than Tony does. If together they weigh 205 pounds, how much will Sarah weigh approximately in kilograms? Assume 1 pound = 0.4535 kilograms.

   a. 41
   b. 48
   c. 50
   d. 52

8. Choose the expression the figure represents.

   a. X ≤ 1
   b. X < 1
   c. X > 1
   d. X ≥ 1

9. Divide 243 by 3^3

   a. 243
   b. 11
   c. 9
   d. 27

10. What fraction of $1500 is $75?

   a. 1/14
   b. 3/5
   c. 7/10
   d. 1/20

11. Below is the attendance for a class of 45.

Day	Number of Absent Students
Monday	5
Tuesday	9
Wednesday	4
Thursday	10
Friday	6

What is the average attendance for the week?

    a. 88%
    b. 85%
    c. 81%
    d. 77%

12. 2/3 − 2/5 =

    a. 4/10
    b. 1/15
    c. 3/7
    d. 4/15

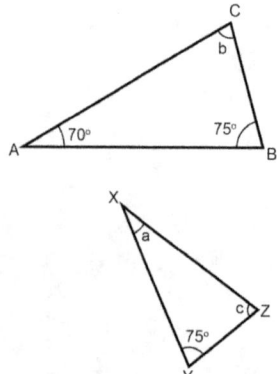

13. What are the respective values of a, b & c if both triangles are similar?

    a. 70°, 70°, 35°
    b. 70°, 35°, 70°
    c. 35°, 35°, 35°
    d. 70°, 75°, 35°

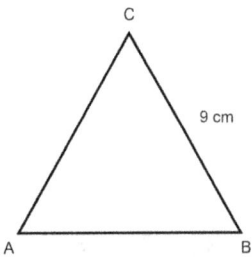

Note: figure not drawn to scale

14. What is the perimeter of the equilateral △ABC above?

    a. 18 cm
    b. 12 cm
    c. 27 cm
    d. 15 cm

15. Express 0.27 + 0.33 as a fraction.

    a. 3/6
    b. 4/7
    c. 3/5
    d. 2/7

16. $7^5 - 3^5 =$

    a. 15,000
    b. 16,564
    c. 15,800
    d. 15,007

17. **What is 2/4 X 3/4 reduced to lowest terms?**

    a. 6/12
    b. 3/8
    c. 6/16
    d. 3/4

18. **Solve the following equation 4(y + 6) = 3y + 30**

    a. y = 20
    b. y = 6
    c. y = 30/7
    d. y = 30

19. **2/3 of 60 + 1/5 of 75 =**

    a. 45
    b. 55
    c. 15
    d. 50

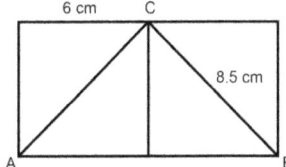

Note: figure not drawn to scale

20. Assuming the 2 quadrangles are identical rectangles, what is perimeter of △ABC in the above shape?

    a. 25.5 cm
    b. 27 cm
    c. 30 cm
    d. 29 cm

21. What is (3.13 + 7.87) X 5?

    a. 65
    b. 50
    c. 45
    d. 55

22. Solve for x if, $10^2 \times 100^2 = 1000^x$

    a. x = 2
    b. x = 3
    c. x = -2
    d. x = 0

23. What is 1/3 of 3/4?

    a. 1/4
    b. 1/3
    c. 2/3
    d. 3/4

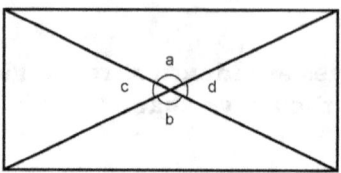

24. What is the sum of all the angles in the rectangle above?

    a. 180°
    b. 360°
    c. 90°
    d. 120°

25. Express 5 x 5 x 5 x 5 x 5 x 5 in exponential form.

    a. 5^6
    b. 10^6
    c. 5^{16}
    d. 5^3

26. Express 9 x 9 x 9 in exponential form and standard form.

    a. $9^3 = 719$
    b. $9^3 = 629$
    c. $9^3 = 729$
    d. $10^3 = 729$

27. If y = 4 and x = 3, solve yx³

    a. -108
    b. 108
    c. 27
    d. 4

28. Divide 0.524 by 10³

    a. 0.0524
    b. 0.00052
    c. 0.00524
    d. 524

29. If X = 7 solve 3x + 5 – 2x

    a. x = 6
    b. x = 12
    c. x = 1
    d. x = 0

30. (x − 2) / 4 − (3x + 5) / 7 = −3, x=?

    a. 6
    b. 7
    c. 10
    d. 13

31. 2/7 + 2/3 =

    a. 12/23
    b. 5/10
    c. 20/21
    d. 6/21

32. $3^2 \times 3^5$

    a. 3^{17}
    b. 3^5
    c. 4^8
    d. 3^7

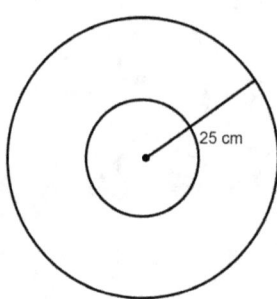

33. **What is the distance traveled by the wheel above, if it makes 175 revolutions?**

    a. 87.5 π m
    b. 875 π m
    c. 8.75 π m
    d. 8750 π m

34. **Expand (x + 7)(x - 3)**

    a. $x^2 + 4x - 21$
    b. x + 21
    c. 2x + 4 - 21
    d. 6x - 21 2x + 4x - 21

35. Estimate 2009 x 108.

   a. 110,000
   b. 2,0000
   c. 21,000
   d. 210,000

Note: figure not drawn to scale

36. A tile factory makes custom tiles, shown above, from two types of stone. If a customer requires 200 tiles, how much black stone will be required?

   a. 256 m²
   b. 2560 m²
   c. 2.56 m²
   d. 25.6 m²

37. Multiply 0.27 by 9^2

   a. 218.7
   b. 21.87
   c. 21
   d. 20.87

38. A woman spent 15% of her income on an item and ends with $120. What percentage of her income is left?

    a. 12%
    b. 85%
    c. 75%
    d. 95%

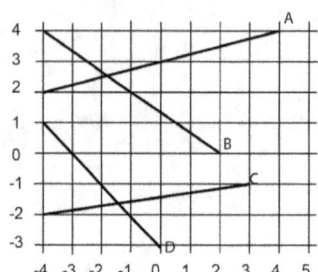

39. Which of the lines above represents the equation 2y − x = 4?

    a. A
    b. B
    c. C
    d. D

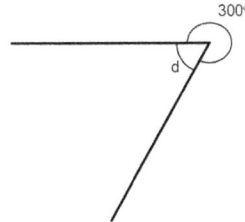

40. What is the measurement of the indicated angle?

    a. 45°
    b. 90°
    c. 60°
    d. 50°

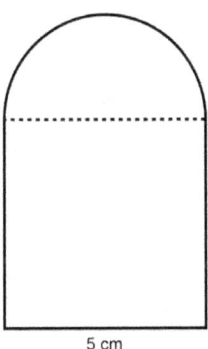

5 cm

Note: figure not drawn to scale

41. What is the perimeter of the above shape?

   a. 22.85 cm
   b. 20 cm
   c. 15 cm
   d. 25.546 cm

42. Solve $3^8/3^5$

   a. 3^3
   b. 3^5
   c. 3^6
   d. 3^4

43. Solve 3x − 27 = 0

   a. x = 24
   b. x = 30
   c. x = 9
   d. x = 21

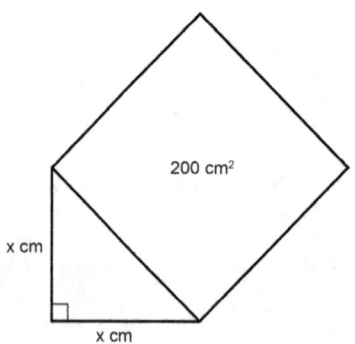

Note: Figure not drawn to scale

44. Assuming the quadrangle in the figure above is square, what is the length of the sides in the triangle above?

    a. 10
    b. 20
    c. 100
    d. 40

45. Solve 3b - 4 + 5b = 0

    a. b = 1
    b. b = 1/3
    c. b = 2
    d. b = 1/2

46. 3.14 + 2.73 + 23.7 =

    a. 28.57
    b. 30.57
    c. 29.56
    d. 29.57

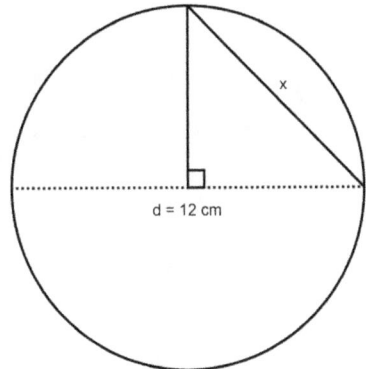

Note: Figure not drawn to scale

47. Calculate the length of side x.

   a. 6.46
   b. 8.48
   c. 3.6
   d. 6.4

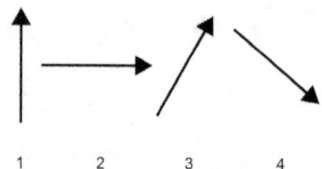

48. What is the correct order of respective slopes for the lines above?

   a. Positive, undefined, negative, positive
   b. Negative, zero, undefined, positive
   c. Undefined, zero, positive, negative
   d. Zero, positive undefined, negative

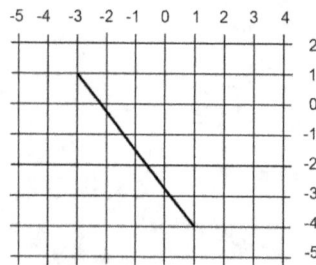

49. What is the slope of the line shown above?

   a. 5/4
   b. -4/5
   c. -5/4
   d. -4/5

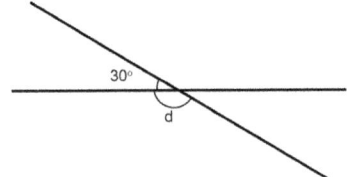

50. What is the indicated angle above?

    a. 150°
    b. 330°
    c. 60°
    d. 120°

Answer Key

Section 1 ☐ Reading

1. A

The correct answer because that fact is stated directly in the passage. The passage explains that Anne taught Helen to hear by allowing her to feel the vibrations in her throat.

2. B

We can infer that Anne is a patient teacher because she did not leave or lose her temper when Helen bit or hit her; she just kept trying to teach Helen. Choice B is incorrect because Anne taught Helen to read and talk. Choice C is incorrect because Anne could hear. She was partially blind, not deaf. Choice D is incorrect because it does not have to do with patience.

3. A

The passage states that it was hard for anyone but Anne to understand Helen when she spoke. Choice A is incorrect because the passage does not mention Helen spoke a foreign language. Choice C is incorrect because there is no mention of how quiet or loud Helen's voice was. Choice D is incorrect because we know from reading the passage that Helen did learn to speak.

4. B

This question tests the reader's summarization skills. The other choices A, B, and C focus on portions of the second paragraph that are too narrow and do not relate to the specific portion of text in question. The complexity of the sentence may mislead students into selecting one of these answers, but rearranging or restating the sentence will lead the reader to the correct answer. In addition, choice A makes an assumption that may or may not be true about the intentions of the company, choice B focuses on one product rather than the idea of the products, and choice C makes an assumption about women that may or may not be true and is not supported by the text.

5. D
This question tests the reader's summarization skills. The question is asking very generally about the message of the passage, and the title, "Ways Characters Communicate in Theater," is one indication of that. The other choices A, B, and C are all directly from the text, and therefore readers may be inclined to select one of them, but are too specific to encapsulate the entirety of the passage and its message.

6. B
The paragraph on soliloquies mentions "To be or not to be," and it is from the context of that paragraph that readers may understand that because "To be or not to be" is a soliloquy, Hamlet will be introspective, or thoughtful, while delivering it. It is true that actors deliver soliloquies alone, and may be "solitary" (choice A), but "thoughtful" (choice B) is more true to the overall idea of the paragraph. Readers may choose C because drama and theater can be used interchangeably and the passage mentions that soliloquies are unique to theater (and therefore drama), but this answer is not specific enough to the paragraph in question. Readers may pick up on the theme of life and death and Hamlet's true intentions and select that he is "hopeless" (choice D), but those themes are not discussed either by this paragraph or passage, as a close textual reading and analysis confirms.

7. C
This question tests the reader's grammatical skills. Choice B seems logical, but parenthesis are actually considered to be a stronger break in a sentence than commas are, and along this line of thinking, actually disrupt the sentence more.

Choices A and D make comparisons between theater and film that are simply not made in the passage, and may or may not be true. This detail does clarify the statement that asides are most unique to theater by adding that it is not completely unique to theater, which may have been why the author didn't chose not to delete it and instead used parentheses to designate the detail's importance (choice C).

8. A
Low blood sugar occurs both in diabetics and healthy adults.

9. B
None of the statements are the author's opinion.

10. A
The author's purpose is the inform.

11. A
The only statement that is not a detail is, "A doctor can diagnosis this medical condition by asking the patient questions and testing."

12. A
This sentence is a recommendation.

13. C
Tips for a good night's sleep is the best alternative title for this article.

14. B
Mental activity is helpful for a good night's sleep is cannot be inferred from this article.

15. A
From the passage, one disadvantage of taking naps is they may keep you awake at night.

16. C
You would you find information about natural selection and adaptation page 110.

17. C
To be infamous means to be remembered for an evil or terrible action. Therefore, the word infamy means to remember a bad or terrible thing. Choice A is incorrect because being famous is not the same as being infamous. Choice B is incorrect because the attack on Pearl Harbor was not good. Choice D is incorrect because Pearl Harbor was not forgotten.

18. C
Each answer choice except choice C contains the name of at least one country that was not part of the AXIS powers.

19. D
It is stated in the passage. Choice A is not correct because there was no indication that Japan would attack San Diego. Choice B is incorrect because the attack on Pearl Harbor was a surprise. Choice C is incorrect because Roosevelt was not planning to attack Japan.

20. C
The passage clearly states that Japan planned a surprise attack. They chose that early time to catch the U.S. military off guard. Choice A is incorrect because the military does not sleep late. Choice B is incorrect because there is no law against bombing countries. Choice D is incorrect because it makes no sense.

21. C
This question tests the reader's vocabulary skills. The uses of the negatives "but" and "less," especially right next to each other, may confuse readers into answering with choices A or D, which list words that are antonyms to "militant." Readers may also be confused by the comparison of healthy people with what is being described as an overly healthy person--both people are good, but the reader may look for which one is "worse" in the comparison, and therefore stray toward the antonym words. The key to understanding the meaning of "militant" is to look at the root of the word; readers can then easily associate it with "military" and gain a sense of what the word signifies: defense (especially considered that the immune system defends the body). Choice C is correct over choice B because "militant" is an adjective, just as the words in choice C are, whereas the words in choice B are nouns.

22. C
This question tests the reader's understanding of function within writing. The other choices are details included surrounding the quoted text, and may therefore confuse the reader. A somewhat contradicts what is said earlier in the paragraph, which is that tests and treatments are improving, and probably doctors are along with them, but the paragraph doesn't actually mention doctors, and the subject of the question is the medicine. Choice B may seem correct to readers who aren't careful to understand that, while the author does mention the large number of people affected, the author is touching on the realities of living with allergies rather than about the likelihood of curing all allergies.

Similarly, while the author does mention the "balance" of the body, which is easily associated with "wholesome," the author is not really making an argument and especially is not making an extreme statement that allergy medicines should be outlawed. Again, because the article's tone is on living with allergies, choice C is an appropriate choice that fits with the title and content of the text.

23. B
This question tests the reader's inference skills. The text does not state who is doing the recommending, but the use of the "patients," as well as the general context of the passage, lends itself to the logical partner, "doctors," choice B. The author does mention the recommendation but doesn't present it as her own (i.e. "I recommend that"), so choice A may be eliminated. It may seem plausible that people with allergies (choice D) may recommend medicines or products to other people with allergies, but the text does not necessarily support this interaction taking place. Choice C may be selected because the EpiPen is specifically mentioned, but the use of the phrase "such as" when it is introduced is not limiting enough to assume the recommendation is coming from its creators.

24. D
This question tests the reader's global understanding of the text. Choice D includes the main topics of the three body paragraphs, and isn't too focused on a specific aspect or quote from the text, as the other questions are, giving a skewed summary of what the author intended. The reader may be drawn to choice B because of the title of the passage and the use of words like "better," but the message of the passage is larger and more general than this.

25. B
Reading the document posted to the Human Resources website is optional.

26. B
The document is recommended changes and have not be implemented yet.

27. C
This question tests the reader's summarization skills. The use of the word "actually" in describing what kind of people poets are, as well as other moments like this, may lead readers to selecting Choices B or D, but the author is more information than trying to persuade readers. The author gives no indication that she loves poetry (choice B) or that people, students specifically (D), should write poems. Choice A is incorrect because the style and content of this paragraph do not match those of a foreword; forewords usually focus on the history or ideas of a specific poem to introduce it more fully and help it stand out against other poems. The author here focuses on several poems and gives broad statements. Instead, she tells a kind of story about poems, giving three very broad time periods in which to discuss them, thereby giving a brief history of poetry, as choice C states.

28. A
This question tests the reader's summarization skills. Key words in the topic sentences of each of the paragraphs ("oldest," "Renaissance," "modern") should give the reader an idea that the author is moving chronologically. The opening and closing sentence-paragraphs are broad and talk generally. B seems reasonable, but epic poems are mentioned in two paragraphs, eliminating the idea that only new types of poems are used in each paragraph. Choice C is also easily eliminated because the author clearly mentions several different poets, groups of people, and poems. Choice D also seems reasonable, considering that the author does move from older forms of poetry to newer forms, but use of "so (that)" makes this statement false, for the author gives no indication that she is rushing (the paragraphs are about the same size) or that she prefers modern poetry.

29. D
This question tests the reader's attention to detail. The key word is "invented"--it ties together the Mesopotamians, who invented the written word, and the fact that they, as the inventors, also invented and used poetry. The other selections focus on other details mentioned in the passage, such as that the Renaissance's admiration of the Greeks (choice C) and that Beowulf is in Old English (choice A). Choice B may seem like an attractive answer because it is unlike the oth-

ers and because the idea of heroes seems rooted in ancient and early civilizations.

30. B
This question tests the reader's vocabulary and contextualization skills. "Telling" is not an unusual word, but it may be used here in a way that is not familiar to readers, as an adjective rather than a verb in gerund form. A may seem like the obvious answer to a reader looking for a verb to match the use they are familiar with. If the reader understands that the word is being used as an adjective and that choice A is a ploy, they may opt to select choice D, "wordy," but it does not make sense in context. Choice C can be easily eliminated, and doesn't have any connection to the paragraph or passage. "Significant" (choice B) makes sense contextually, especially relative to the phrase "give insight" used later in the sentence.

VOCABULARY

31. C
Dauntless: adj. Invulnerable to fear or intimidation.

32. A
Juxtaposed: adj. Placed side-by-side often for comparison or contrast.

33. B
Regicide: v. killing of a king.

34. A
Pernicious: adj. Causing much harm in a subtle way.

35. A
Immune: adj. Resistant to a particular infection or toxin owing to the presence of specific antibodies.

36. B
Nimble: adj. Quick and light in movement or action.

37. A
Queries: n. Questions or inquiries.

38. C
Depose: To remove (a leader) from (high) office, without killing the incumbent.

39. D
Pedestrian: Ordinary, dull; everyday; unexceptional.

40. B
Petulant: adj. Childishly irritable.

41. D
Pesticide: n. A substance used for destroying insects or other organisms harmful to cultivated plants or to animals.

42. D
Salient: adj. worthy or note or relevant.

43. B
Sedentary: adj. not moving or sitting in one place.

44. A
Famine: n. extreme scarcity of food.

45. A
Stint: n. To be sparing.

46. A
Precipitate: v. to rain.

47. C
Edify: v. To instruct or improve morally or intellectually.

48. B
Egress: n. An exit or way out.

49. A
Recede: v. To move back, to move away.

50. A
Confidential: adj. kept secret within a certain circle of persons; not intended to be known publicly.

English Language Arts

1. C
Comma separate phrases.

2. D
The comma separates clauses and numbers are separated with a comma. The correct sentence is,
'To travel around the globe, you have to drive 25,000 miles.'

3. A
The dog loved chasing bones, but never ate them; it was running that he enjoyed.

4. B
The semicolon links independent clauses with a conjunction (therefore).

5. D
The third conditional is used for talking about an unreal situation (that did not happen) in the past. For example, "If I had studied harder, [if clause] I would have passed the exam [main clause]. Which is the same as, "I failed the exam, because I didn't study hard enough."

6. C
Double negative sentence. In double negative sentences, one negative is replaced with "any."

7. A
Disagreeing with a negative statement uses "neither." Disagreeing with a negative statement uses "neither." Use "I do" and "He does."

8. C
Doesn't, does not, or does is used with the third person singular--words like he, she, and it. Don't, do not, or do is used for other subjects.

9. C
Bring vs. Take. Usage depends on your location. Something coming your way is brought to you. Something going away is taken from you.

10. C
Present perfect. You cannot use the Present Perfect with specific time expressions such as: yesterday, one year ago, last week, when I was a child, at that moment, that day, one day, etc. The Present Perfect is used with unspecific expressions such as: ever, never, once, many times, several times, before, so far, already, yet, etc.

11. C
Fewer vs. Less. 'Fewer' is used with countables and 'less' is used with uncountables.

12. B
Went vs. Gone. Went is the simple past tense. Gone is used in the past perfect.

13. A
When using 'however,' place a comma before and after, except when however begins the sentence.

14. C
Its vs. It's. 'It's' is a contraction for it is or it has. 'Its' is a possessive pronoun meaning, more or less, of it or belonging to it.

15. C
Lay vs. Lie. Lie requires an object and lay does not. Laid is the past tense of lay.

16. D
The third conditional is used for talking about an unreal situation (that did not happen) in the past. For example,

"If I had studied harder, [if clause] I would have passed the exam [main clause]. Which is the same as, "I failed the exam, because I didn't study hard enough."

17. D
A vs. An. The article 'a' come before a consonant and 'an' comes before a vowel.

18. A
Accept vs. Except. To accept is to receive or to say yes. Except is a preposition that means excluding.

19. A
Advise vs. Advice. To advise is to give advice. Advice is an opinion that someone offers.

20. C
Adapt vs. Adopt.
Adapt means "to change." Usually we adapt to someone or something. Adopt means "to take as one's own."

21. D
Among vs. Between. 'Among' is for more than 2 items, and 'between' is only for 2 items.

When he's among friends (many or more than 2), Robert seems confident, but, between you and me (two), he is very shy.

22. D
At vs. About. At refers to a specific time and about refers to a more general time. A common usage is 'at about 10,' but it isn't proper grammar.

23. B
Beside vs. Besides. 'Beside' means next to, and 'besides' means in addition to.

24. A
Can vs. May. 'Can' refers to ability and 'may' refers to permission.

Although John can swim (is able to. very well, he may not (permission. be allowed to swim in the pool.

25. B
Continual vs. Continuous. 'Continuous' means a time with no interruption and 'continual' means a time with interruption.

Her continual absences (with interruption – not always absent) caused a continuous disruption (the disruption was ongoing without interruption) at the office.

26. A
Emigrate vs. Immigrate. To emigrate means to leave one's country and to immigrate means to come to a country.

27. B
Further vs. Farther. 'Farther' is used for physical distance, and 'further' is used for figurative distance.

28. B
Former vs. Latter. 'Former' refers to the first of two things, 'latter' to the second.

29. A
Sit vs. Set. 'Set' requires an object – something to set down. 'Sit' is something that you do, like sit on the chair.

30. C
The names of God, specific deities, religious figures, and holy books are capitalized.

31. B
Capitalize a title when used with a name or other noun. So, The Mayor of Chicago is capitalized, whereas "he spoke to the mayor" is not.

32. B
Titles preceding names are capitalized, but not titles that follow names.

33. C
Holidays are capitalized, the names of seasons are not.

34. C
The names of seasons are not capitalized because they are generic nouns. If a season is used in a title, such as the "Fall 2012 semester," Fall 2012 is a title and capitalized.

35. A
A Pronoun should conform to its antecedent in gender, number and person.

36. A
The verb LAY should always take an object. Here the subject is the table. The three forms of the verb lay are: lay, laid and laid. The sentence above is in past tense.

37. B
Use the singular verb form when nouns are qualified with "every" or "each," even if they are joined by 'and.'

38. B
The sentence is correct. Use a plural verb for nouns like measles, tongs, trousers, riches, scissors etc.

39. B
Use "could," the past tense of "can" to express ability or capacity.

40. C
The sentence is correct. Words such as neither, each, many, either, every, everyone, everybody and any should take a singular pronoun.

41. A
The verb "ought" expresses desirability, duty and probability. The verb is usually followed by "to."

42. A
When two subjects are linked with "with" or "as well," use the verb form that matches the first subject.

43. A
When you use 'each other' it should be used for two things or people. When you use 'one another' it should be used for things and people above two

44. B
The verb rise ('to go up', 'to ascend.') can appear in three forms, rise, rose, and risen. The verb should not take an object.

45. A
The sentence is correct. Use "whom" in the objective case, and use "who" a subjective case.

46. C
Always use the singular verb form for nouns like politics, wages, mathematics, innings, news, advice, summons, furniture, information, poetry, machinery, vacation, scenery etc.

47. B
Use a singular verb with a proper noun in plural form that refers to a single entity. Here the The World Health Organization is a single entity, although it is made up on many members.

48. A
Will is used in the second or third person (they, he, she and you), while shall is used in the first person (I and we). Both verbs are used to express futurity.

MATHEMATICS

1. B
Six times a number plus five is the same as saying six times (a number plus five). Or,
6 * (a number plus five). Let X be the number so, 6(X+5).

2. A
Three plus a number times 7 equals 42. Let X be the number. (3 + X) times 7 = 42
7(3 + X) = 42

3. C
If there are 5 friends and each drink costs $1.89, we can round up to $2 per drink and estimate the total cost at, 5 X $2 = $10.

The actual cost is 5 X $1.89 = $9.45.

4. B
Estimate 215 X 65. First start with 200 X 50, which is 10,000, so the answer will be about 10,000. The only choice that is close is 13,500, choice B.

5. A
The graph shows oil consumption peaked in 2011.

6. A
The sample space of this event will be S = { (H,1),(H,2),(H,3),(H,4),(H,5),(H,6) (T,1),(T,2),(T,3),(T,4),(T,5),(T,6) } So there are a total of 12 outcomes and 8 winning outcomes. The probability of a win in a single event is P (W) =8/12=2/3. In 20 games the probability of a win = 2/3 × 20 = 13.53, or about 13.

7. D
Let us denote Sarah's weight by "x." Then, since she weighs 25 pounds more than Tony, Tony will be x-25. They together weigh 205 pounds which means that the sum of the two representations will be equal to 205:

Sarah : x

Tony : x - 25

x + (x - 25) = 205 ... by arranging this equation we have:

x + x - 25 = 205

2x - 25 = 205 ... we add 25 to each side to have x term alone:

2x - 25 + 25 = 205 + 25

2x = 230

x = 230/2

x = 115 pounds → Sarah weighs 115 pounds. Since 1 pound is 0.4535 kilograms, we need to multiply 115 by 0.4535 to have her weight in kilograms:

x = 115 * 0.4535 = 52.1525 kilograms → this is equal to 52 when rounded to the nearest whole number.

8. B
The line is pointing towards numbers less than 1. The equation is therefore, X < 1.

9. C
$243/3^3$ 3 x 3 x 3 = 27
243/27 = 9

10. D
75/1500 = 15/300 = 3/60 = 1/20

11. B

Day	Number of Absent Students	Number of Present Students	% Attendance
Monday	5	40	88.88%
Tuesday	9	36	80.00%
Wednesday	4	41	91.11%
Thursday	10	35	77.77%
Friday	6	39	86.66%

88.88 + 80.00 + 91.11 + 77.77 + 86.66/5
424.42/5 = 84.88
Round up to 85%.

Percentage attendance will be 85%

12. D
2/3 - 2/5 = 10 - 6 /15 = 4/15

13. D
Comparing respective angles - 70°, 75°, 35°

14. C
Equilateral triangle with 9 cm. sides
Perimeter = 9 + 9 + 9 = 27 cm.

15. C
0.27 + 0.33 = 0.60 and 0.60 = 60/100 = 3/5

16. B
(7 x 7 x 7 x 7 x 7) - (3 x 3 x 3 x 3 x 3) = 16,807 – 243 = 16,564

17. B
2/4 X 3/4 = 6/16, and reduced to the lowest terms = 3/8

18. B
4y + 24 = 3y + 30, = 4y – 3y + 24 = 30, = y + 24 = 30, = y = 30 – 24, = y = 6

19. B
2/3 x 60 = 40 and 1/5 x 75 = 15, 40 + 15 = 55.

20. D
Perimeter of triangle ABC is asked.
Perimeter of a triangle = sum of the three sides.

Here, Perimeter of $\triangle ABC$ = |AC| + |CB| + |AB|.

Since the triangle is located in the middle of two adjacent and identical rectangles, we find the side lengths using these rectangles:

|AB| = 6 + 6 = 12 cm

|CB| = 8.5 cm

|AC| = |CB| = 8.5 cm

Perimeter = |AC| + |CB| + |AB| = 8.5 + 8.5 + 12 = 29 cm

21. D
3.13 + 7.87 = 11 and 11 X 5 = 55

22. A
10 x 10 x 100 x 100 = 1000^x, =100 x 10,000 = 1000^x, = 1,000,000 = 1000^x = x = 2

23. A
1/3 X 3/4 = 3/12 = 1/4

24. B
a + b + c + d = ?
The sum of angles around a point is 360°
a + b + c + d = 360°

25. A
5^6

26. C
Exponential form is 9^3 and standard from is 729

27. B
$(4)(3)^3$ = (4)(27) = 108

28. B
0.524/ 10 x 10 x 10 = 0.524/1000 = 0.000524

29. B
X = 7, so 3x = 3 x 7 = 21, 2x = 2 x 7 = 14, so 21 + 5 - 14 = 26 - 14 = 12

30. C
There are two fractions containing x and the denominators are different. First, let us find a common denominator to simplify the expression. The least common multiplier of 4 and 7 is 28. Then,
7(x – 2) / 28 – 4(3x + 5) / 28 = -3.28 / 28 ... Since both sides are written on the denominator 28 now, we can eliminate them:
7(x – 2) – 4(3x + 5) = -84
7x – 14 – 12x – 20 = -84
-5x = - 84 + 14 + 20
-5x = - 50
x = 50/5
x = 10

31. C
2/7 + 2/3 = 6+14 /21 (21 is the common denominator) = 20/21

32. D
When multiplying exponents with the same base, add the exponents. $3^2 \times 3^5 = 3^{2+5} = 3^7$

33. A
The wheel travels 2πr distance when it makes one revolution. Here, r stands for the radius. The radius is given as 25 cm in the figure. So,

2πr = 2π * 25 = 50π cm is the distance traveled in one revolution.

In 175 revolutions: 175 * 50π = 8750π cm is traveled.

We are asked to find the distance in meter.

1 m = 100 cm So;

8750π cm = 8750π / 100 = 87.5π m

34. A
Multiply the first bracket and the second. x^2 - 3x + 7x -21= x^2 + 4x – 21

35. D
2009 X 108 = 216,972.   This is an easy question to guess. 2000 X 100 = 200,000, so choices A, B and C can be eliminated right away.

36. A
Black stone for 200 tiles = 200 x [Total tile area – Inner white area(4 triangles)]
= 200 x [(16^2)-(4 x 1/2 x 8 x 8)] = 200 x (256 - 128) = 200 x 128 = 25600 cm²
Converting to meters – 1 cm. = 0.01 meters
= 25600/100 m²
= 256 m²

37. B
0.27 (9 x 9) = 0.27 x 81 = 21.87

38. B
She spent 15% - 100% - 15% = 85%

39. A

If a line represents an equation, all points on that line should satisfy the equation. Meaning that all (x, y) pairs present on the line should be able to verify that 2y - x is equal to 4. We can find out the correct line by trying a (x, y) point existing on each line. It is easier to choose points on the intersection of the gridlines:

Let us try the point (4, 4) on line A:

2 * 4 - 4 = 4

8 - 4 = 4

4 = 4 ... this is a correct result, so the equation for line A is 2y - x = 4.

Let us try other points to check the other lines:

Point (-1, 2) on line B:

2 * 2 - (-1) = 4

4 + 1 = 4

5 = 4 ... this is a wrong result, so the equation for line B is not 2y - x = 4.

Point (3, -1) on line C:

2 * (-1) - 3 = 4

-2 - 3 = 4

-5 = 4 ... this is a wrong result, so the equation for line C is not 2y - x = 4.

Point (-2, -1) on line D:

2 * (-1) - (-2) = 4

-2 + 2 = 4

0 = 4 ... this is a wrong result, so the equation for line D is not 2y - x = 4.

40. C
The sum of angles around a point is 360°
d + 300 = 360°
d = 60°

41. A
Find the perimeter of a shape made by merging a square and a semi circle. Perimeter = 3 sides of the square + 1/2 circumference of the circle.
= (3 x 5) + 1/2 (5 π)
= 15 + 2.5 π
= 15 + 7.853975
Perimeter = 22.85 cm

42. A
$3^{8-5} = 3^3$
To divide exponents with the same base, subtract the exponents.

43. C
3x = 27, x = 27/3, x = 9

44. A
If we call one side of the square "a," the area of the square will be a^2.

We know that $a^2 = 200$ cm².

On the other hand; there is an isosceles right triangle. Using the **Pythagorean Theorem:**

(Hypotenuse)² = (Adjacent Side)² + (Opposite Side)² Where the hypotenuse is equal to one side of the square. So,

$a^2 = x^2 + x^2$

$200 = 2x^2$

$200/2 = 2x^2/2$

$100 = x^2$

$x = \sqrt{100}$

x = 10 cm

45. D
3b + 5b − 4, = 8b − 4, = 8b = 4, b = 4/8, = b = ½

46. D
3.14 + 2.73 = 5.87 and 5.87 + 23.7 = 29.57

47. B
In the question, we have a right triangle formed inside the circle. We are asked to find the length of the hypotenuse of this triangle. We can find the other two sides of the triangle by using circle properties:

The diameter of the circle is equal to 12 cm. The legs of the right triangle are the radii of the circle; so they are 6 cm long.

Using the Pythagorean Theorem:

(Hypotenuse)² = (Adjacent Side)² + (Opposite Side)²

$x^2 = r^2 + r^2$

$x^2 = 6^2 + 6^2$

$x^2 = 72$

$x = \sqrt{72}$

$x = 8.48$

48. C
Undefined, zero, positive, negative.

49. C
Slope (m) = change in y / change in x

$(x_1, y_1) = (-3, 1)$ & $(x_2, y_2) = (1, -4)$
Slope = [−4 − 1]/[1−(−3)] = −5/4

50. A
The angles opposite both angles 30° and angle d are respectively equal to vertical angles.
2(30° + d) = 360°
2d = 360° − 60°
2d = 300°
d = 150°

PRACTICE TEST QUESTIONS SET 2

THE PRACTICE TEST PORTION PRESENTS QUESTIONS THAT ARE REPRESENTATIVE OF THE TYPE OF QUESTION YOU SHOULD EXPECT TO FIND ON THE CHSPE. HOWEVER, THEY ARE NOT INTENDED TO MATCH EXACTLY WHAT IS ON THE CHSPE.

For the best results, take this Practice Test as if it were the real exam. Set aside time when you will not be disturbed, and a location that is quiet and free of distractions. Read the instructions carefully, read each question carefully, and answer to the best of your ability.

Use the bubbles provided. When you have completed the Practice Test, check your answer against the Answer Key and read the explanation provided.

READING

	A	B	C	D	E		A	B	C	D	E
1	○	○	○	○	○	26	○	○	○	○	○
2	○	○	○	○	○	27	○	○	○	○	○
3	○	○	○	○	○	28	○	○	○	○	○
4	○	○	○	○	○	29	○	○	○	○	○
5	○	○	○	○	○	30	○	○	○	○	○
6	○	○	○	○	○	31	○	○	○	○	○
7	○	○	○	○	○	32	○	○	○	○	○
8	○	○	○	○	○	33	○	○	○	○	○
9	○	○	○	○	○	34	○	○	○	○	○
10	○	○	○	○	○	35	○	○	○	○	○
11	○	○	○	○	○	36	○	○	○	○	○
12	○	○	○	○	○	37	○	○	○	○	○
13	○	○	○	○	○	38	○	○	○	○	○
14	○	○	○	○	○	39	○	○	○	○	○
15	○	○	○	○	○	40	○	○	○	○	○
16	○	○	○	○	○	41	○	○	○	○	○
17	○	○	○	○	○	42	○	○	○	○	○
18	○	○	○	○	○	43	○	○	○	○	○
19	○	○	○	○	○	44	○	○	○	○	○
20	○	○	○	○	○	45	○	○	○	○	○
21	○	○	○	○	○	46	○	○	○	○	○
22	○	○	○	○	○	47	○	○	○	○	○
23	○	○	○	○	○	48	○	○	○	○	○
24	○	○	○	○	○	49	○	○	○	○	○
25	○	○	○	○	○	50	○	○	○	○	○

English and Language Arts

	A B C D E		A B C D E
1	○ ○ ○ ○ ○	26	○ ○ ○ ○ ○
2	○ ○ ○ ○ ○	27	○ ○ ○ ○ ○
3	○ ○ ○ ○ ○	28	○ ○ ○ ○ ○
4	○ ○ ○ ○ ○	29	○ ○ ○ ○ ○
5	○ ○ ○ ○ ○	30	○ ○ ○ ○ ○
6	○ ○ ○ ○ ○	31	○ ○ ○ ○ ○
7	○ ○ ○ ○ ○	32	○ ○ ○ ○ ○
8	○ ○ ○ ○ ○	33	○ ○ ○ ○ ○
9	○ ○ ○ ○ ○	34	○ ○ ○ ○ ○
10	○ ○ ○ ○ ○	35	○ ○ ○ ○ ○
11	○ ○ ○ ○ ○	36	○ ○ ○ ○ ○
12	○ ○ ○ ○ ○	37	○ ○ ○ ○ ○
13	○ ○ ○ ○ ○	38	○ ○ ○ ○ ○
14	○ ○ ○ ○ ○	39	○ ○ ○ ○ ○
15	○ ○ ○ ○ ○	40	○ ○ ○ ○ ○
16	○ ○ ○ ○ ○	41	○ ○ ○ ○ ○
17	○ ○ ○ ○ ○	42	○ ○ ○ ○ ○
18	○ ○ ○ ○ ○	43	○ ○ ○ ○ ○
19	○ ○ ○ ○ ○	44	○ ○ ○ ○ ○
20	○ ○ ○ ○ ○	45	○ ○ ○ ○ ○
21	○ ○ ○ ○ ○	46	○ ○ ○ ○ ○
22	○ ○ ○ ○ ○	47	○ ○ ○ ○ ○
23	○ ○ ○ ○ ○	48	○ ○ ○ ○ ○
24	○ ○ ○ ○ ○	49	○ ○ ○ ○ ○
25	○ ○ ○ ○ ○	50	○ ○ ○ ○ ○

MATHEMATICS

	A	B	C	D	E		A	B	C	D	E
1	○	○	○	○	○	26	○	○	○	○	○
2	○	○	○	○	○	27	○	○	○	○	○
3	○	○	○	○	○	28	○	○	○	○	○
4	○	○	○	○	○	29	○	○	○	○	○
5	○	○	○	○	○	30	○	○	○	○	○
6	○	○	○	○	○	31	○	○	○	○	○
7	○	○	○	○	○	32	○	○	○	○	○
8	○	○	○	○	○	33	○	○	○	○	○
9	○	○	○	○	○	34	○	○	○	○	○
10	○	○	○	○	○	35	○	○	○	○	○
11	○	○	○	○	○	36	○	○	○	○	○
12	○	○	○	○	○	37	○	○	○	○	○
13	○	○	○	○	○	38	○	○	○	○	○
14	○	○	○	○	○	39	○	○	○	○	○
15	○	○	○	○	○	40	○	○	○	○	○
16	○	○	○	○	○	41	○	○	○	○	○
17	○	○	○	○	○	42	○	○	○	○	○
18	○	○	○	○	○	43	○	○	○	○	○
19	○	○	○	○	○	44	○	○	○	○	○
20	○	○	○	○	○	45	○	○	○	○	○
21	○	○	○	○	○	46	○	○	○	○	○
22	○	○	○	○	○	47	○	○	○	○	○
23	○	○	○	○	○	48	○	○	○	○	○
24	○	○	○	○	○	49	○	○	○	○	○
25	○	○	○	○	○	50	○	○	○	○	○

READING AND LANGUAGE ARTS

Questions 1 - 4 refer to the following passage.

Passage 1 - The Crusades

In 1095 Pope Urban II proclaimed the First Crusade with the intent and stated goal to restore Christian access to holy places in and around Jerusalem. Over the next 200 years there were 6 major crusades and numerous minor crusades in the fight for control of the "Holy Land." Historians are divided on the real purpose of the Crusades, some believing that it was part of a purely defensive war against Islamic conquest; some see them as part of a long-running conflict at the frontiers of Europe; and others see them as confident, aggressive, papal-led expansion attempts by Western Christendom. The impact of the crusades was profound, and judgment of the Crusaders ranges from laudatory to highly critical. However, all agree that the Crusades and wars waged during those crusades were brutal and often bloody. Several hundred thousand Roman Catholic Christians joined the Crusades, they were Christians from all over Europe.

Europe at the time was under the Feudal System, so while the Crusaders made vows to the Church they also were beholden to their Feudal Lords. This led to the Crusaders not only fighting the Saracen, the commonly used word for Muslim at the time, but also each other for power and economic gain in the Holy Land. This infighting between the Crusaders is why many historians hold the view that the Crusades were simply a front for Europe to invade the Holy Land for economic gain in the name of the Church. Another factor contributing to this theory is that while the army of crusaders marched towards Jerusalem they pillaged the land as they went. The church and feudal Lords vowing to return the land to its original beauty, and inhabitants, this rarely happened though as the Lords often kept the land for themselves. A full 800 years after the Crusades, Pope John Paul II expressed his sorrow for the massacre of innocent people and the lasting damage the Medieval church caused in that area of the World.

Practice Test Questions 2

1. What is the tone of this article?

    a. Subjective

    b. Objective

    c. Persuasive

    d. None of the Above

2. What can all historians agree on concerning the Crusades?

    a. It achieved great things

    b. It stabilized the Holy Land

    c. It was bloody and brutal

    d. It helped defend Europe from the Byzantine Empire

3. What impact did the feudal system have on the Crusades?

    a. It unified the Crusaders

    b. It helped gather volunteers

    c. It had no effect on the Crusades

    d. It led to infighting, causing more damage than good

4. What does Saracen mean?

    a. Muslim

    b. Christian

    c. Knight

    d. Holy Land

Questions 5 - 8 refer to the following passage.

ABC Electric Warranty

ABC Electric Company warrants that its products are free from defects in material and workmanship. Subject to the conditions and limitations set forth below, ABC Electric will, at its option, either repair or replace any part of its products that prove defective due to improper workmanship or materials.

This limited warranty does not cover any damage to the product from improper installation, accident, abuse, misuse, natural disaster, insufficient or excessive electrical supply, abnormal mechanical or environmental conditions, or any unauthorized disassembly, repair, or modification.

This limited warranty also does not apply to any product on which the original identification information has been altered, or removed, has not been handled or packaged correctly, or has been sold as second-hand.

This limited warranty covers only repair, replacement, refund or credit for defective ABC Electric products, as provided above.

5. I tried to repair my ABC Electric blender, but could not, so can I get it repaired under this warranty?

    a. Yes, the warranty still covers the blender

    b. No, the warranty does not cover the blender

    c. Uncertain. ABC Electric may or may not cover repairs under this warranty

6. My ABC Electric fan is not working. Will ABC Electric provide a new one or repair this one?

    a. ABC Electric will repair my fan

    b. ABC Electric will replace my fan

    c. ABC Electric could either replace or repair my fan can request either a replacement or a repair.

7. My stove was damaged in a flood. Does this warranty cover my stove?

    a. Yes, it is covered.

    b. No, it is not covered.

    c. It may or may not be covered.

    d. ABC Electric will decide if it is covered

8. Which of the following is an example of improper workmanship?

    a. Missing parts

    b. Defective parts

    c. Scratches on the front

    d. None of the above

Questions 9 – 12 refer to the following passage.

Passage 2 - Women and Advertising

Only in the last few generations have media messages been so widespread and so readily seen, heard, and read by so many people. Advertising is an important part of both selling and buying anything from soap to cereal to jeans. For whatever reason, more consumers are women than are men. Media message are subtle but powerful, and more attention has been paid lately to how these message affect women. Of all the products that women buy, makeup, clothes, and other stylistic or cosmetic products are among the most popular. This means that companies focus their advertising on women, promising them that their product will make her feel, look, or smell better than the next company's product will. This competition has resulted in advertising that is more and more ideal and less and less possible for everyday women. However, because women do look to these ideals and the products they represent as how they can potentially become, many women have developed unhealthy attitudes about themselves when they have failed to become those ideals.

In recent years, more companies have tried to change advertisements to be healthier for women. This includes featuring models of more sizes and addressing a huge outcry against unfair tools such as airbrushing and photo editing. There is debate about what the right balance between real and ideal is, because fashion is also considered art and some changes are made to purposefully elevate fashionable products and signify that they are creative, innovative, and the work of individual people. Artists want their freedom protected as much as women do, and advertising agencies are often caught in the middle.

Some claim that the companies who make these changes are not doing enough. Many people worry that there are still not enough models of different sizes and different ethnicities. Some people claim that companies use this healthier type of advertisement not for the good of women, but because they would like to sell products to the women who are looking for these kinds of messages. This is also a hard balance to find: companies do need to make money, and women do need to feel respected.

While the focus of this change has been on women, advertising can also affect men, and this change will hopefully be a lesson on media for all consumers.

9. The second paragraph states that advertising focuses on women

      a. to shape what the ideal should be

      b. because women buy makeup

      c. because women are easily persuaded

      d. because of the types of products that women buy

10. According to the passage, fashion artists and female consumers are at odds because

   a. there is a debate going on and disagreement drives people apart

   b. both of them are trying to protect their freedom to do something

   c. artists want to elevate their products above the reach of women

   d. women are creative, innovative, individual people

11. The author uses the phrase "for whatever reason" in this passage to

   a. keep the focus of the paragraph on media messages and not on the differences between men and women

   b. show that the reason for this is unimportant

   c. argue that it is stupid that more women are consumers than men

   d. show that he or she is tired of talking about why media messages are important

12. This passage suggests that

   a. advertising companies are still working on making their messages better

   b. all advertising companies seek to be more approachable for women

   c. women are only buying from companies that respect them

   d. artists could stop producing fashionable products if they feel bullied

Questions 13 - 16 refer to the following passage.

FDR, the Treaty of Versailles, and the Fourteen Points

At the conclusion of World War I, those who had won the war and those who were forced to admit defeat welcomed the end of the war and expected that a peace treaty would be signed. The American president, Franklin D. Roosevelt, played an important part in proposing what the agreements should be and did so through his Fourteen Points.
World War I had begun in 1914 when an Austrian archduke was assassinated, leading to a domino effect that pulled the world's most powerful countries into war on a large scale. The war catalyzed the creation and use of deadly weapons that had not previously existed, resulting in a great loss of soldiers on both sides of the fighting. More than 9 million soldiers were killed.

The United States agreed to enter the war right before it ended, and many believed that its decision to become finally involved brought on the end of the war. FDR made it very clear that the U.S. was entering the war for moral reasons and had an agenda focused on world peace. The Fourteen Points were individual goals and ideas (focused on peace, free trade, open communication, and self reliance) that FDR wanted the power nations to strive for now that the war had concluded. He was optimistic and had many ideas about what could be accomplished through and during the post-war peace. However, FDR's fourteen points were poorly received when he presented them to the leaders of other world powers, many of whom wanted only to help their own countries and to punish the Germans for fueling the war, and they fell by the wayside. World War II was imminent, for Germany lost everything.

Some historians believe that the other leaders who participated in the Treaty of Versailles weren't receptive to the Fourteen Points because World War I was fought almost entirely on European soil, and the United States lost much less than did the other powers. FDR was in a unique position to determine the fate of the war, but doing it on his own terms did not help accomplish his goals. This is only one historical example of how the United State has tried to use its power as an important country, but found itself limited because of geological or ideological factors.

13. The main idea of this passage is that

    a. World War I was unfair because no fighting took place in America

    b. World War II happened because of the Treaty of Versailles

    c. the power the United States has to help other countries also prevents it from helping other countries

    d. Franklin D. Roosevelt was one of the United States' smartest presidents

14. According to the second paragraph, World War I started because

    a. an archduke was assassinated

    b. weapons that were more deadly had been developed

    c. a domino effect of allies agreeing to help each other

    d. the world's most powerful countries were large

15. The author includes the detail that 9 million soldiers were killed

    a. to demonstrate why European leaders were hesitant to accept peace

    b. to show the reader the dangers of deadly weapons

    c. to make the reader think about which countries lost the most soldiers

    d. to demonstrate why World War II was imminent

16. According to this passage, the word catalyzed means

    a. analyzed

    b. sped up

    c. invented

    d. funded

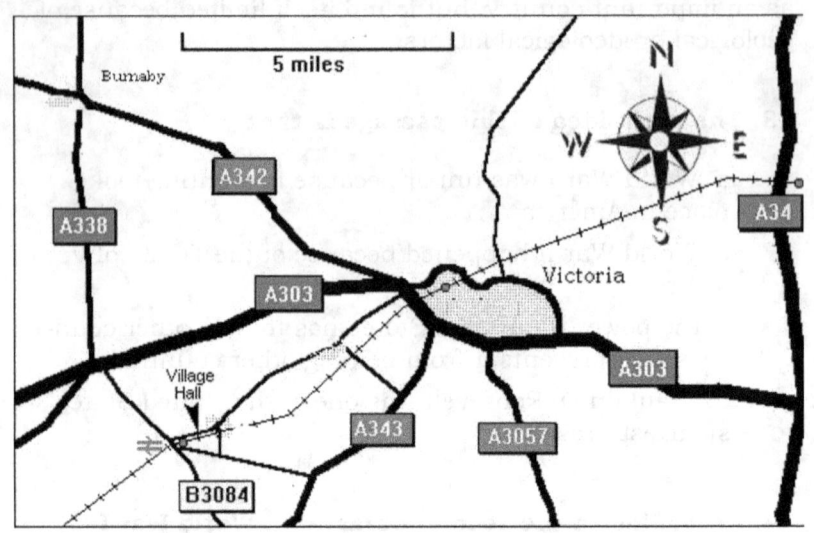

17. Approximately how far is Victoria to Burnaby?

    a. About 10 miles
    b. About 5 miles
    c. About 15 miles
    d. About 20 miles

18. How is the Village Hall from Victoria?

    a. About 10 miles
    b. About 5 miles
    c. About 15 miles
    d. About 20 miles

Questions 19 - 22 refer to the following passage.

Chocolate Chip Cookies

3/4 cup sugar
3/4 cup packed brown sugar
1 cup butter, softened
2 large eggs, beaten
1 teaspoon vanilla extract
2 1/4 cups all-purpose flour
1 teaspoon baking soda
3/4 teaspoon salt
2 cups semisweet chocolate chips
If desired, 1 cup chopped pecans, or chopped walnuts.
Preheat oven to 375 degrees.

Mix sugar, brown sugar, butter, vanilla and eggs in a large bowl. Stir in flour, baking soda, and salt. The dough will be very stiff.

Stir in chocolate chips by hand with a sturdy wooden spoon. Add the pecans, or other nuts, if desired. Stir until the chocolate chips and nuts are evenly dispersed.

Drop dough by rounded tablespoonfuls 2 inches apart onto a cookie sheet.

Bake 8 to 10 minutes or until light brown. Cookies may look underdone, but they will finish cooking after you take them out of the oven.

19. What is the correct order for adding these ingredients?

    a. Brown sugar, baking soda, chocolate chips
    b. Baking soda, brown sugar, chocolate chips
    c. Chocolate chips, baking soda, brown sugar
    d. Baking soda, chocolate chips, brown sugar

20. What does sturdy mean?

    a. Long
    b. Strong
    c. Short
    d. Wide

21. What does disperse mean?

    a. Scatter
    b. To form a ball
    c. To stir
    d. To beat

22. When can you stop stirring the nuts?

    a. When the cookies are cooked.
    b. When the nuts are evenly distributed.
    c. When the nuts are added.
    d. After the chocolate chips are added.

Questions 23 - 26 refer to the following passage.

Passage 5 - Frankenstein

Great God! What a scene has just taken place! I am yet dizzy with the remembrance of it. I hardly know whether I shall have the power to detail it; yet the tale which I have recorded would be incomplete without this final and wonderful catastrophe. I entered the cabin where lay the remains of my ill-fated and admirable friend. Over him hung a form which I cannot find words to describe—gigantic in stature, yet uncouth and distorted in its proportions. As he hung over the coffin, his face was concealed by long locks of ragged hair; but one vast hand was extended, in color and apparent texture like that of a mummy. When he heard the sound of my approach, he ceased to utter exclamations of grief and horror and sprung towards the window. Never did I behold a vision so horrible as his face, of such loathsome yet appalling hideousness. I shut my eyes involuntarily and endeavored to recollect what were my duties with regard to this destroyer. I called on him to stay.

He paused, looking on me with wonder, and again turning towards the lifeless form of his creator, he seemed to forget my presence, and every feature and gesture seemed instigated by the wildest rage of some uncontrollable passion.

"That is also my victim!" he exclaimed. "In his murder my crimes are consummated; the miserable series of my being is wound to its close! Oh, Frankenstein! Generous and self-devoted being! What does it avail that I now ask thee to pardon me? I, who irretrievably destroyed thee by destroying all thou lovedst. Alas! He is cold, he cannot answer me."

His voice seemed suffocated, and my first impulses, which had suggested to me the duty of obeying the dying request of my friend in destroying his enemy, were now suspended by a mixture of curiosity and compassion. I approached this tremendous being; I dared not again raise my eyes to his face, there was something so scaring and unearthly in his ugliness. I attempted to speak, but the words died away on my lips. The monster continued to utter wild and incoherent self-reproaches. At length I gathered resolution to address him in a pause of the tempest of his passion.

"Your repentance," I said, "is now superfluous. If you had listened to the voice of conscience and heeded the stings of remorse before you had urged your diabolical vengeance to this extremity, Frankenstein would yet have lived." [7]

23. Who is the "ill-fated and admirable friend" who is lying in the coffin?

    a. Frankenstein's monster

    b. Frankenstein

    c. Mary Shelley

    d. Unknown

24. Why is the speaker 'suspended" from following through on his duty to destroy the monster?

    a. The way the monster looks

    b. The monster's remorse

    c. Curiosity and compassion

    d. Fear the monster might kill him too

25. How does Frankenstein's monster destroy Frankenstein?

    a. By killing Frankenstein

    b. By letting himself be the monster everyone sees him as

    c. By destroying everything Frankenstein loved

    d. All of the above

26. When the Speaker says the monster's repentance is "superfluous, what does he mean?

    a. That it is unnecessary and unused because Frankenstein is already dead and cannot hear him

    b. That he accepts the repentance on behalf of Frankenstein

    c. That the monster does not actually feel remorseful

    d. That his repentance is unneeded because he did not do anything wrong

Questions 27 - 29 refer to the following passage.

Lowest Price Guarantee

Get it for less. Guaranteed!

ABC Electric will beat any advertised price by 10% of the difference.

    1) If you find a lower advertised price, we will beat it by 10% of the difference.

2) If you find a lower advertised price within 30 days* of your purchase we will beat it by 10% of the difference.

3) If our own price is reduced within 30 days* of your purchase, bring in your receipt and we will refund the difference.

*14 days for computers, monitors, printers, laptops, tablets, cellular & wireless devices, home security products, projectors, camcorders, digital cameras, radar detectors, portable DVD players, DJ and pro-audio equipment, and air conditioners.

27. I bought a radar detector 15 days ago and saw an ad for the same model only cheaper. Can I get 10% of the difference refunded?

    a. Yes. Since it is less than 30 days, you can get 10% of the difference refunded.

    b. No. Since it is more than 14 days, you cannot get 10% of the difference re-funded.

    c. It depends on the cashier.

    d. Yes. You can get the difference refunded.

28. I bought a flat-screen TV for $500 10 days ago and found an advertisement for the same TV, at another store, on sale for $400. How much will ABC refund under this guarantee?

    a. $100

    b. $110

    c. $10

    d. $400

29. What is the purpose of this passage?

    a. To inform
    b. To educate
    c. To persuade
    d. To entertain

Questions 30 refers to the following passage.

Passage 6 - What Is Mardi Gras?

Mardi Gras is fast becoming one of the South's most famous and most celebrated holidays. The word Mardi Gras comes from the French and the literal translation is "Fat Tuesday." The holiday has also been called Shrove Tuesday, due to its associations with Lent. The purpose of Mardi Gras is to celebrate and enjoy before the Lenten season of fasting and repentance begins.

What originated by the French Explorers in New Orleans, Louisiana in the 17th century is now celebrated all over the world. Panama, Italy, Belgium and Brazil all host large scale Mardi Gras celebrations, and many smaller cities and towns celebrate this fun loving Tuesday as well. Usually held in February or early March, Mardi Gras is a day of extravagance, a day for people to eat, drink and be merry, to wear costumes, masks and to dance to jazz music.
The French explorers on the Mississippi River would be in shock today if they saw the opulence of the parades and floats that grace the New Orleans streets during Mardi Gras these days. Parades in New Orleans are divided by organizations. These are more commonly known as Krewes.

Being a member of a Krewe is quite a task because Krewes are responsible for overseeing the parades. Each Krewe's parade is ruled by a Mardi Gras "King and Queen." The role of the King and Queen is to "bestow" gifts on their adoring fans as the floats ride along the street. They throw doubloons, which is fake money and usually colored green, purple and gold, which are the colors of Mardi Gras. Beads in those color shades are also thrown and cups are thrown as well. Beads are by far the most popular souvenir of any Mardi Gras parade, with each spectator attempting to gather as many as possible.

30. The purpose of Mardi Gras is to

    a. Repent for a month.

    b. Celebrate in extravagant ways.

    c. Be a member of a Krewe.

    d. Explore the Mississippi.

VOCABULARY

31. Choose the adjective that means shocking, terrible or wicked.

    a. Pleasantries

    b. Heinous

    c. Shrewd

    d. Provencal

32. Choose the noun that means a person of thing that tells or announces the coming of someone or something.

    a. Harbinger

    b. Evasion

    c. Bleak

    d. Craven

33. Choose a word that means the same as the underlined word.

He wasn't especially generous. All the servings were very <u>judicious</u>.

    a. Abundant
    b. Careful
    c. Sparing
    d. Careless

34. Because of the growing use of _____ as a fuel, corn production has greatly increased.

    a. Alcohol
    b. Ethanol
    c. Natural gas
    d. Oil

35. In heavily industrialized areas, the pollution of the air causes many to develop _____ diseases.

    a. Respiratory
    b. Cardiac
    c. Alimentary
    d. Circulatory

36. Choose the best definition of inherent.

    a. To receive money in a will
    b. An essential part of
    c. To receive money from a will
    d. None of the above

37. Choose the best vapid.

a. adj. tasteless or bland

b. v. To inflict, as a revenge or punishment

c. v. to convert into gas

d. v. to go up in smoke

38. Choose the best definition of waif.

a. n. a sick and hungry child

b. n. an orphan staying in a foster home

c. n. homeless child or stray

d. n. a type of French bread eaten with cheese

39. Choose the adjective that means similar or identical.

a. Soluble

b. Assembly

c. Conclave

d. Homologous

40. Choose a word with the same meaning as the underlined word.

We used that operating system 20 years ago, now it is obsolete.

a. Functional

b. Disused

c. Obese

d. None of the Above

41. Choose the word with the same meaning as the underlined word

His bad manners really <u>rankle</u> me.

  a. Annoy
  b. Obsolete
  c. Enliven
  d. None of the above

42. Because hydroelectric power is a _____ source of energy, its use is excellent for the environment.

  a. Significant
  b. Disposable
  c. Renewable
  d. Reusable

43. Choose the best definition of torpid.

  a. Fast
  b. Rapid
  c. Sluggish
  d. Violent

44. Choose the best definition of gregarious.

  a. Sociable
  b. Introverted
  c. Large
  d. Solitary

45. Choose the best definition of mutation.

   a. v. To utter with a loud and vehement voice
   b. n. change or alteration
   c. n. An act or exercise of will
   d. v. To cause to be one

46. Choose the best definition of lithe.

   a. adj. small in size
   b. adj. Artificial
   c. adj. flexible or plaint
   d. adj. fake

47. Choose the best definition of resent.

   a. adj. To express displeasure or indignation
   b. v. To cause to be one
   c. adj. Clumsy
   d. adj. strong feelings of love

48. Choose and adjective that means irrelevant or not having substance or matter

   a. Immaterial
   b. Prohibition
   c. Prediction
   d. Brokerage

49. Choose and adjective that means perfect, no faults or errors.

    a. Impeccable
    b. Formidable
    c. Genteel
    d. Disputation

50. Choose the best definition of pudgy.

    a. v. to draw general inferences
    b. Adj. fat, plump and overweight
    c. n. permanence
    d. adj. spoilt or bad condition

English Grammar, Punctuation, Capitalization and Usage.

1. Jessica's father was in the Navy, so she attended schools in Newark; New Jersey, Key West; Florida, San Diego, California, and Fairbanks, Alaska.

    a. Jessica's father was in the Navy, so she attended schools in Newark, New Jersey, Key   West, Florida, San Diego, California, and Fairbanks, Alaska.

    b. Jessica's father was in the Navy, so she attended schools in: Newark, New Jersey, Key West, Florida, San Diego, California, and Fairbanks, Alaska.

    c. Jessica's father was in the Navy, so she attended schools in Newark, New Jersey; Key West, Florida; San Diego, California; and Fairbanks, Alaska.

    d. None of the choices are correct.

2. George wrecked John's <u>car; that</u> was the end of their friendship.

    a. George wrecked John's car that was the end of their friendship.

    b. George wrecked John's car. that was the end of their friendship.

    c. The sentence is correct.

    d. None of the choices are correct.

3. The dress was not Gina's <u>favorite, however,</u> she wore it to the dance.

    a. The dress was not Gina's favorite; however, she wore it to the dance.

    b. None of the choices are correct.

    c. The dress was not Gina's favorite, however; she wore it to the dance.

    d. The dress was not Gina's favorite however, she wore it to the dance.

4. Chris showed his dedication to golf in many <u>ways; for example,</u> he watched all the tournaments on television.

    a. Chris showed his dedication to golf in many ways, for example, he watched all the tournaments on television.

    b. The sentence is correct.

    c. Chris showed his dedication to golf in many ways, for example; he watched all the tournaments on television.

    d. Chris showed his dedication to golf in many ways for example he watched all the tournaments on television.

5. There was scarcely <u>no food</u> in the pantry, because <u>not nobody</u> ate at home.

    a. There was scarcely no food in the pantry, because nobody ate at home.

    b. There was scarcely any food in the pantry, because nobody ate at home.

    c. There was scarcely any food in the pantry, because not nobody ate at home.

    d. The sentence is correct.

6. Choose the sentence with the correct grammar.

    a. If Joe had told me the truth, I wouldn't have been so angry.

    b. If Joe would have told me the truth, I wouldn't have been so angry.

    c. I wouldn't have been so angry if Joe would have told the truth.

    d. If Joe would have telled me the truth, I wouldn't have been so angry.

7. Michael <u>have lived</u> in that house for forty years, while I <u>has owned</u> this one for only six weeks.

    a. Michael has lived in that house for forty years, while I has owned this one for only six weeks.

    b. Michael have lived in that house for forty years, while I have owned this one for only six weeks.

    c. None of the choices are correct.

    d. Michael has lived in that house for forty years, while I have owned this one for only six weeks.

8. Until you <u>take</u> the overdue books to the library, you can't <u>take</u> any new ones home.

    a. Until you take the overdue books to the library, you can't take any new ones home

    b. Until you take the overdue books to the library, you can't bring any new ones home.

    c. Until you bring the overdue books to the library, you can't take any new ones home.

    d. None of the choices are correct.

9. If they had <u>gone</u> to the party, he would have <u>gone</u> too.

    a. The sentence is correct.

    b. If they had went to the party, he would have gone too.

    c. If they had gone to the party, he would have went too.

    d. If they had went to the party, he would have went too.

10. His doctor suggested that he eat <u>fewer</u> snacks and do <u>fewer</u> lounging on the couch.

    a. His doctor suggested that he eat less snacks and do fewer lounging on the couch.

    b. His doctor suggested that he eat fewer snacks and do less lounging on the couch.

    c. His doctor suggested that he eat less snacks and do less lounging on the couch.

    d. None of the choices are correct.

11. Lee pronounced it's name incorrectly; it's an impatiens, not an impatience.

   a. The sentence is correct.

   b. Lee pronounced its name incorrectly; its an *impatiens*, not an *impatience*.

   c. Lee pronounced it's name incorrectly; its an *impatiens*, not an *impatience*.

   d. Lee pronounced its name incorrectly; it's an *impatiens*, not an *impatience*.

12. There was, however very little difference between the two.

   a. There was however, very little difference between the two.

   b. None of the choices are correct.

   c. There was; however, very little difference between the two.

   d. There was, however, very little difference between the two.

13. The Ford Motor Company was named for Henry Ford

   a. which had founded the company.

   b. who founded the company.

   c. whose had founded the company.

   d. whom had founded the company.

14. Thomas Edison _____ after he invented the light bulb, television, motion pictures, and phonograph.

   a. has always been known as the greatest inventor

   b. was always been known as the greatest inventor

   c. must have had been always known as the greatest inventor

   d. will had been known as the greatest inventor

15. The weatherman on Channel 6 said that this has been the _____ .

   a. most hottest summer on record.

   b. hottest summer on record.

   c. hotter summer on record.

   d. None of the above

16. Although Joe is tall for his age, his brother Elliot is _____ of the two.

   a. the tallest

   b. more tallest

   c. the tall

   d. the taller

17. I can never remember how to use those two common words, "sell," meaning to trade a product for money, or _____ meaning an event where products are traded for less money than usual.

   a. sale-

   b. "sale,"

   c. "sale

   d. "to sale,"

18. His father is

   a. a poet and novelist

   b. poet and novelist

   c. a poet and a novelist

   d. none of the above

19. The class just finished reading , _____ a short story by Carl Stephenson about a plantation owner's battle with army ants.

    a. -"Leinengen versus the Ants,"

    b. Leinengen versus the Ants,

    c. "Leinengen versus the Ants,"

    d. Leinengen versus the Ants

20. After the car was fixed it _____ again.

    a. ran good

    b. ran well

    c. would have run well

    d. ran more well

21. "Where does the sun go during the _____ asked little Kathy.

    a. night,"

    b. night?",

    c. night,?"

    d. night?"

22. Vegetables are a <u>healthy</u> food; eating them can make you more <u>healthy</u>.

    a. Vegetables are a healthy food; eating them can make you more healthful.

    b. Vegetables are a healthful food; eating them can make you more healthful.

    c. None of the choices are correct.

    d. Vegetables are a healthful food; eating them can make you more healthy.

23. When James went <u>in</u> his room, he found that his clothes had been put <u>in</u> the closet.

    a. When James went into his room, he found that his clothes had been put in the closet.

    b. None of the choices are correct.

    c. When James went into his room, he found that his clothes had been put into the closet.

    d. When James went in his room, he found that his clothes had been put into the closet.

24. After you lay the books on the counter, you may lay down for a nap.

    a. The sentence is correct.

    b. After you lie the books on the counter, you may lay down for a nap.

    c. After you lay the books on the counter, you may lie down for a nap.

    d. After you lay the books on the counter, you may lay down for a nap.

25. Don <u>would never of thought</u> of that book, but you <u>could have reminded</u> him.

    a. Don would never have thought of that book, but you could have reminded him.

    b. None of the choices are correct.

    c. Don would never have thought of that book, but you could of have reminded him.

    d. Don would never of thought of that book, but you could of reminded him.

26. Mrs. Foster <u>learned</u> me many things, but I was <u>taught</u> the most by Mr. Wallace.

    a. Mrs. Foster taught me many things, but I learned the most from Mr. Wallace.

    b. The sentence is correct.

    c. Mrs. Foster learned me many things, but I learned the most from Mr. Wallace.

    d. None of the choices are correct.

27. He did not have to <u>loose</u> the race; if only his shoes weren't so <u>loose</u>!

    a. He did not have to loose the race; if only his shoes weren't so lose!

    b. He did not have to lose the race; if only his shoes weren't so loose!

    c. The sentence is correct.

    d. None of the choices are correct.

28. The attorney did not want to <u>prosecute</u> the defendant; his goal was to <u>prosecute</u> the guilty party.

    a. None of the choices are correct.

    b. The attorney did not want to persecute the defendant; his goal was to persecute the guilty party.

    c. The attorney did not want to prosecute the defendant; his goal was to persecute the guilty party.

    d. The attorney did not want to persecute the defendant; his goal was to prosecute the guilty party.

29. The speeches must <u>proceed</u> the election; the election cannot <u>proceed</u> without hearing from the candidates.

    a. The speeches must precede the election; the election cannot proceed without hearing from the candidates.

    b. The speeches must precede the election; the election cannot precede without hearing from the candidates.

    c. The speeches must proceed the election; the election cannot precede without hearing from the candidates.

    d. The sentence is correct.

30. My best friend said, "Always Count your Change."

    a. My best friend said, "always count your change."

    b. The sentence is correct.

    c. My best friend said, "Always count your change."

    d. None of the choices are correct.

31. The <u>Victorian Era</u> was in the <u>nineteenth century</u>.

    a. The sentence is correct.

    b. The victorian era was in the nineteenth century.

    c. The Victorian Era was in the Nineteenth century.

    d. The Victorian era was in the Nineteenth century.

32. I prefer <u>pepsi</u> to <u>Coke</u>.

    a. I prefer pepsi to coke.

    b. The sentence is correct.

    c. I prefer Pepsi to Coke.

    d. None of the choices are correct.

33. I always have <u>french fries</u> with my <u>coke</u>.

    a. The sentence is correct.
    b. I always have french fries with my Coke.
    c. I always have French Fries with my Coke.
    d. None of the choices are correct.

34. The <u>blue Jays</u> are my favorite team.

    a. The blue jays are my favorite team.
    b. The sentence is correct.
    c. The Blue Jays are my favorite team.
    d. None of the choices are correct.

35. The <u>Southwest</u> is the best part of the country.

    a. The sentence is correct.
    b. The southwest is the best part of the country.
    c. The southwest is the best part of the Country.
    d. None of the choices are correct.

MATHEMATICS

1. Translate the following into an equation:

2 plus a number divided by 7.

    a. $(2 + X)/7$
    b. $(7 + X)/2$
    c. $(2 + 7)/X$
    d. $2/(7 + X)$

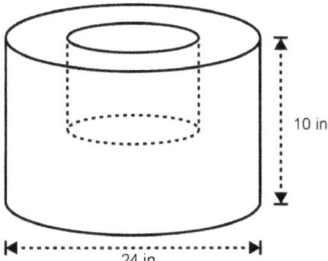

Note: figure not drawn to scale

2. What is the volume of the above solid made by a hollow cylinder that is half the size (in all dimensions) of the larger cylinder?

    a. 1440 π in³
    b. 1260 π in³
    c. 1040 π in³
    d. 960 π in³

3. If a train travels at 72 kilometers per hour, how far will it travel in 12 seconds?

    a. 200 m
    b. 220 m
    c. 240 m
    d. 260 m

4. Tony bought 15 dozen eggs for $80. 16 eggs were broken during loading and unloading. He sold the remaining eggs for $0.54 each. What will be his percent profit?

    a. 11%
    b. 11.2%
    c. 11.5%
    d. 12%

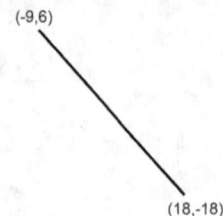

5. What is the slope of the line above?

    a. -8/9
    b. 9/8
    c. -9/8
    d. 8/9

6. In a class of 83 students, 72 are present. What percent of students are absent?

    a. 12%
    b. 13%
    c. 14%
    d. 15%

7. $9ab^2 + 8ab^2 =$

    a. ab^2
    b. $17ab^2$
    c. 17
    d. $17a^2b^2$

8. The total expense of building a fence around a square shaped field is $2000 at a rate of $5 per meter. What is the length of one side?

    a. 80 meters

    b. 100 meters

    c. 40 meters

    d. 320 meters

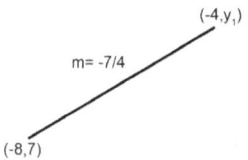

9. With the data given above, what is the value of y_1?

    a. 0

    b. -7

    c. 7

    d. 8

10. In a local election at polling station A, 945 voters cast their vote out of 1270 registered voters. At polling station B, 860 cast their vote out of 1050 registered voters and at station C, 1210 cast their vote out of 1440 registered voters. What was the total turnout including all three polling stations?

    a. 70%

    b. 74%

    c. 76%

    d. 80%

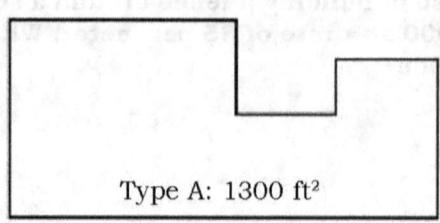

Type A: 1300 ft²

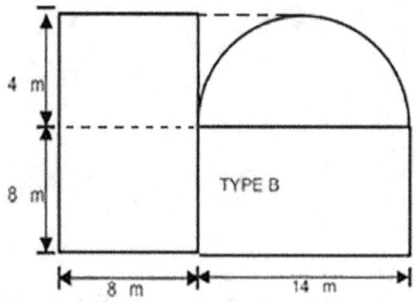

Note: Figure not drawn to scale

11. The price of houses in a certain subdivision is based on the total area. Susan is watching her budget and wants to choose the house with the lowest area. Which house type, A (1300 ft2) or B, should she choose if she would like the house with the lowest price? (1 m2 = 10.76 ft2 & π = 22/7)

    a. Type B is smaller at 140 ft²
    b. Type A is smaller
    c. Type B is smaller at 855 ft²
    d. Type B is larger

Consider the following graph.

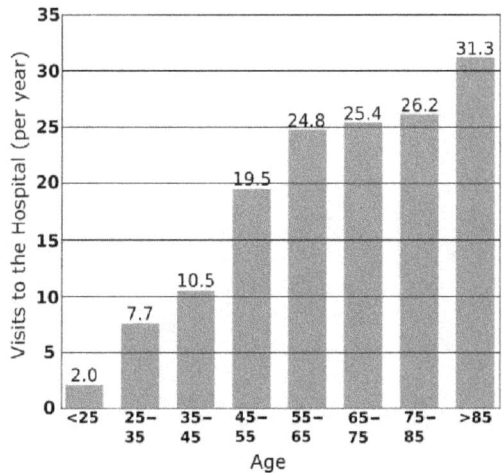

12. How many hospital visits per year does a person aged 85 or more make?

    a. 26.2

    b. 31.3

    c. More than 31.3

    d. A decision cannot be made from this graph.

13. Based on this graph, how many visits per year do you expect a person that is 95 or older to make?

    a. More than 31.3

    b. Less than 31.3

    c. 31.3

    d. A decision cannot be made from this graph.

14. How much water can be stored in a cylindrical container 5 meters in diameter and 12 meters high?

Note: figure not drawn to scale

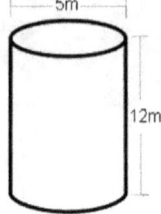

a. 235.65 m³
b. 223.65 m³
c. 240.65 m³
d. 252.65 m³

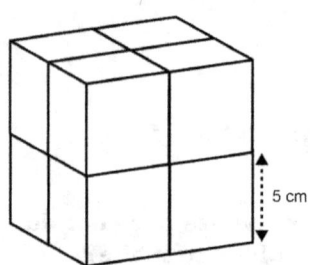

Note: figure not drawn to scale

15. Assuming the figure above has cubes, what is the volume?

a. 125 cm³
b. 875 cm³
c. 1000 cm³
d. 500 cm³

16. Choose the expression the figure represents.

    a. X > 2
    b. X ≥ 2
    c. X < 2
    d. X ≤ 2

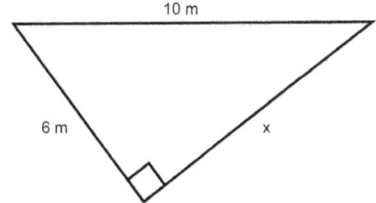

Note: figure not drawn to scale

17. What is the length of the missing side in the triangle above?

    a. 6
    b. 4
    c. 8
    d. 5

18. 60 is 75% of x. Solve for x.

    a. 80
    b. 90
    c. 75
    d. 70

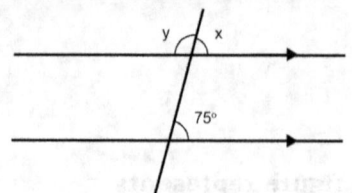

19. What is the value of the angle y?

a. 25°
b. 15°
c. 30°
d. 105°

20. Express 71/1000 as a decimal.

a. .71
b. .0071
c. .071
d. 7.1

21. .33 × .59 =

a. .1947
b. 1.947
c. .0197
d. .1817

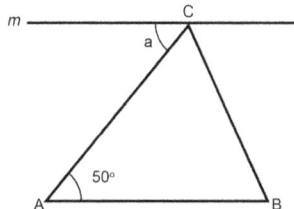

Note: Figure not drawn to scale

22. If the line *m* is parallel to the side AB of △ABC, what is angle *a*?

    a. 130°
    b. 25°
    c. 65°
    d. 50°

23. 7x − 9 = 47. Solve for x.

    a. 8
    b. 7
    c. 9
    d. 6

24. What number is in the ten thousandths place in 1.7389

    a. 1
    b. 8
    c. 9
    d. 3

25. .87 - .48 =

a. .39
b. .49
c. .41
d. .37

26. Which is the equivalent decimal number for forty nine thousandths?

a. .49
b. .0049
c. .049
d. 4.9

27. Which of the following is not a fraction equivalent to 3/4?

a. 6/8
b. 9/12
c. 12/18
d. 21/28

28. Which one of the following is greater than a third?

a. 84/231
b. 6/35
c. 3/22
d. b and c

29. Which of the following numbers is the greatest?

a. 1
b. $\sqrt{2}$
c. 3/2
d. 4/3

30. 2b + 9b − 5b = 0

    a. 3b
    b. 6b
    c. 4b
    d. 8b

31. $(4Y^3 - 2Y^2) + (7Y^2 + 3y - y) =$

    a. $4y^3 + 9y^2 + 4y$
    b. $5y^3 + 5y^2 + 3y$
    c. $4y^3 + 7y^2 + 2y$
    d. $4y^3 + 5y^2 + 2y$

32. 4.7 + .9 + .01 =

    a. 5.5
    b. 6.51
    c. 5.61
    d. 5.7

33. 7(2y + 8) + 1 − 4(y + 5) =

    a. 10y + 36
    b. 10y + 77
    c. 18y + 37
    d. 10y + 37

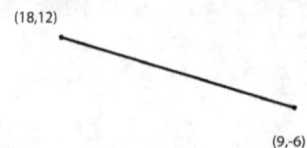

34. What is the distance between the two points?

   a. ≈19
   b. 20
   c. ≈21
   d. ≈22

35. 60% of x is 12. Solve for x.

   a. 18
   b. 15
   c. 25
   d. 20

36. .84 ÷ .7 =

   a. .12
   b. 12
   c. .012
   d. 1.2

37. 6(x − 4) = 3x + 12. Solve for x.

   a. 15
   b. 8
   c. 12
   d. 14

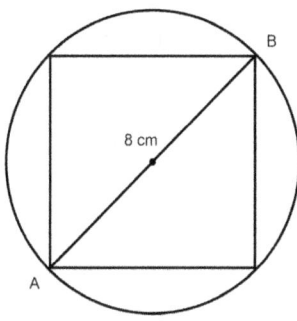

Note: figure not drawn to scale

38. What is area of the circle?

    a. 4 π cm²
    b. 12 π cm²
    c. 10 π cm²
    d. 16 π cm²

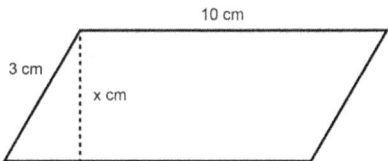

Note: figure not drawn to scale

39. What is the perimeter of the parallelogram above?

    a. 12 cm
    b. 26 cm
    c. 13 cm
    d. (13+x) cm

40. Richard gives 's' amount of salary to each of his 'n' employees weekly. If he has 'x' amount of money then how many days he can employ these 'n' employees.

    a. sx/7n
    b. 7x/nx
    c. nx/7s
    d. 7x/ns

41. Express 87% as a decimal.

    a. .087
    b. 8.7
    c. .87
    d. 87

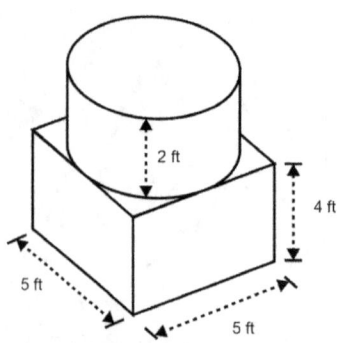

Note: figure not drawn to scale

42. What is the approximate total volume of the above solid?

    a. 120 ft^3
    b. 100 ft^3
    c. 140 ft^3
    d. 160 ft^3

43. Susan wants to buy a leather jacket that costs $545.00 and is on sale for 10% off. What is the approximate cost?

    a. $525
    b. $450
    c. $475
    d. $500

44. Translate the following into an equation:

Five greater than 3 times a number.

    a. 3X + 5
    b. 5X + 3
    c. (5 + 3)X
    d. 5(3 + X)

45. What is the slope of the line above?

    a. 1
    b. 2
    c. 3
    d. -2

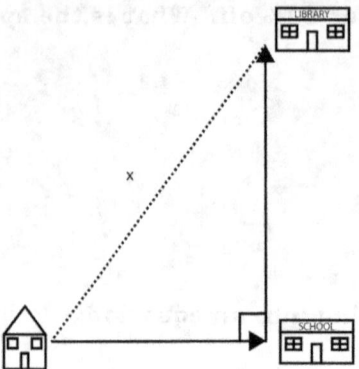

Note: figure not drawn to scale

46. Every day starting from his home Peter travels due east 3 kilometers to the school. After school he travels due north 4 kilometers to the library. What is the distance between Peter's home and the library?

    a. 15 km
    b. 10 km
    c. 5 km
    d. 12 ½ km

47. The cost of waterproofing canvas is .50 per square yard. What is the total cost for waterproofing a canvas truck cover that is 15' x 24'?

    a. $18.00
    b. $6.67
    c. $180.00
    d. $20.00

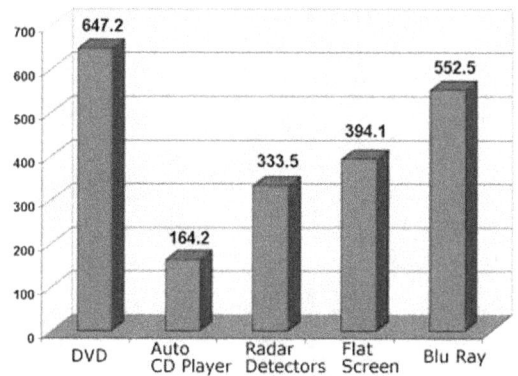

48. Consider the graph above. What is the third best-selling product?

    a. Radar Detectors
    b. Flat Screen TV
    c. Blu Ray
    d. Auto CD Players

49. Which two products are the closest in the number of sales?

    a. Blu Ray and Flat Screen TV
    b. Flat Screen TV and Radar Detectors
    c. Radar Detectors and Auto CD Players
    d. DVD players and Blu Ray

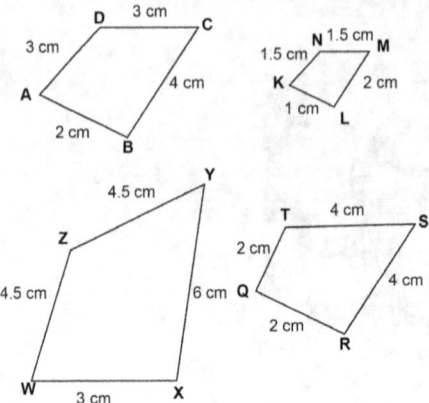

50. Which of the above quadrilaterals are similar?

a. All are similar
b. QRST, KLMN, WXYZ
c. ABCD, KLMN, WXYZ
d. None of the choices are correct.

Answer Key

Reading Comprehension

1. A
Choice B is incorrect; the author did not express their opinion on the subject matter. Choice C is incorrect, the author was not trying to prove a point, nor is the author trying to persuade.

2. C
Choice C is correct; historians believe it was brutal and bloody. Choice A is incorrect; there is no consensus that the Crusades achieved great things. Choice B is incorrect; it did not stabilize the Holy Lands. Choice D is incorrect, some historians do believe this was the purpose but not all historians.

3. D
The feudal system led to infighting. Choice A is incorrect, it had the opposite effect. Choice B is incorrect, though this is a good answer, it is not the best answer. The Church asked for volunteers not the Feudal Lords. Choice C is incorrect, it did have an effect on the Crusades.

4. A
Saracen was a generic term for Muslims widely used in Europe during the later medieval era.

5. B
This warranty does not cover a product that you have tried to fix yourself. From paragraph two, "This limited warranty does not cover ... any unauthorized disassembly, repair, or modification. "

6. C
ABC Electric could either replace or repair the fan, provided the other conditions are met. ABC Electric has the option to repair or replace.

7. B
The warranty does not cover a stove damaged in a flood.

From the passage, "This limited warranty does not cover any damage to the product from improper installation, accident, abuse, misuse, natural disaster, insufficient or excessive electrical supply, abnormal mechanical or environmental conditions."

A flood is an "abnormal environmental condition," and a natural disaster, so it is not covered.

8. A
A missing part is an example of defective workmanship. This is an error made in the manufacturing process. A defective part is not considered workmanship.

9. D
This question tests the reader's summarization skills. The other choices A, B, and C focus on portions of the second paragraph that are too narrow and do not relate to the specific portion of text in question. The complexity of the sentence may mislead students into selecting one of these answers, but rearranging or restating the sentence will lead the reader to the correct answer. In addition, choice A makes an assumption that may or may not be true about the intentions of the company, choice B focuses on one product rather than the idea of the products, and choice C makes an assumption about women that may or may not be true and is not supported by the text.

10. B
This question tests reader's attention to detail. If a reader selects A, he or she may have picked up on the use of the word "debate" and assumed, very logically, that the two are at odds because they are fighting; however, this is simply not supported in the text. Choice C also uses very specific quotes from the text, but it rearranges and gives them false meaning. The artists want to elevate their creations above the creations of other artists, thereby showing that they are "creative" and "innovative." Similarly, choice D takes phrases straight from the text and rearranges and confuses them. The artists are described as wanting to be "creative, innovative, individual people," not the women.

11. A

This question tests reader's vocabulary and summarization skills. This phrase, used by the author, may seem flippant and dismissive if readers focus on the word "whatever" and misinterpret it as a popular, colloquial term. In this way, Choices B and C may mislead the reader to selecting one of them by including the terms "unimportant" and "stupid," respectively. Choice D is a similar misreading, but doesn't make sense when the phrase is at the beginning of the passage and the entire passage is on media messages. Choice A is literally and contextually appropriate, and the reader can understand that the author would like to keep the introduction focused on the topic the passage is going to discuss.

12. A

This question tests a reader's inference skills. The extreme use of the word "all" in choice B suggests that every single advertising company are working to be approachable, and while this is not only unlikely, the text specifically states that "more" companies have done this, signifying that they have not all participated, even if it's a possibility that they may some day. The use of the limiting word "only" in choice C lends that answer similar problems; women are still buying from companies who do not care about this message, or those companies would not be in business, and the passage specifies that "many" women are worried about media messages, but not all. Readers may find choice D logical, especially if they are looking to make an inference, and while this may be a possibility, the passage does not suggest or discuss this happening. Choice A is correct based on specifically because of the relation between "still working" in the answer and "will hopefully" and the extensive discussion on companies struggles, which come only with progress, in the text.

13. C

This question tests the reader's summarization skills. The entire passage is leading up to the idea that the president of the US may not have had grounds to assert his Fourteen Points when other countries had lost so much. Choice A is pretty directly inferred by the text, but it does not adequately summarize what the entire passage is trying to communicate. Choice B may also be inferred by the passage when it says that the war is "imminent," but it does not represent the entire message, either. The passage does seem to be in praise of FDR, or at least in respect of him, but it does not in any way claim that he is the smartest president, nor does this represent the many other points included. Choice C is then the obvious answer, and most directly relates to the closing sentences which it rewords.

14. C
This question tests the reader's attention to detail. The passage does state that choices A and B are true, and while those statements are in proximity to the explanation for why the war started, they are not the reason given. Choice D is a mix up of words used in the passage, which says that the largest powers were in play but not that this fact somehow started the war. The passage does make a direct statement that a domino effect started the war, supporting choice C as the correct answer.

15. A
This question tests the reader's understanding of functions in writing. Throughout the passage, it states that leaders of other nations were hesitant to accept generous or peaceful terms because of the grievances of the war, and the great loss of life was chief among these. While the passage does touch on the devastation of deadly weapons (B), the use of this raw, emotional fact serves a larger purpose, and the focus of the passage is not weapons. While readers may indeed consider who lost the most soldiers (C) when, so many countries were involved and the inequalities of loss are mentioned in the passage, there is no discussion of this in the passage. Choice D is related to A, but choice A is more direct and relates more to the passage.

16. B
This question tests the reader's vocabulary skills. Choice A may seem appealing to readers because it is phonetically similar to "catalyzed," but the two are not related in any other way. Choice C makes sense in context, but if plugged in to the sentence creates a redundancy that doesn't make sense. Choice D does also not make sense contextually, even if the reader may consider that funds were needed to create more weaponry, especially if it was advanced.

17. A
Victoria is about 5 miles from Burnaby.

18. B
The Village Hall is about 5 miles from Victoria.

19. A
The correct order of ingredients is brown sugar, baking soda and chocolate chips.

20. B
Sturdy: strong, solid in structure or person. In context, Stir in chocolate chips by hand with a *sturdy* wooden spoon.

21. A
Disperse: to scatter in different directions or break up. In context, Stir until the chocolate chips and nuts are evenly *dispersed*.

22. B
You can stop stirring the nuts when they are evenly distributed. From the passage, "Stir until the chocolate chips and nuts are evenly dispersed."

23. B
Choice A is incorrect as the Monster killed Frankenstein, not the other way around. Choice B is correct, Frankenstein is dead. Choice C is incorrect - Mary Shelley is the author. Choice D is incorrect, the person is called Frankenstein.

24. C
The speaker 'suspended' from following through on his duty to destroy the monster due to curiosity and compassion. The other choices may seem reasonable, but are not explicitly given in the passage.

25. D
All the choices are correct. Frankenstein's monster destroys Frankenstein by

    a. By killing Frankenstein

    b. By letting himself be the monster everyone sees him as

    c. By destroying everything Frankenstein loved

26. A
Superfluous means unnecessary. Looking at the context of the word as it is used in the passage:

"Your repentance," I said, "is now superfluous. If you had listened to the voice of conscience and heeded the stings of remorse before you had urged your diabolical vengeance to this extremity, Frankenstein would yet have lived."

27. B
The time limit for radar detectors is 14 days. Since you made the purchase 15 days ago, you do not qualify for the guarantee.

28. B
Since you made the purchase 10 days ago, you are covered by the guarantee. Since it is an advertised price at a different store, ABC Electric will "beat" the price by 10% of the difference, which is,

500 – 400 = 100 – difference in price

100 X 10% = $10 – 10% of the difference

The advertised lower price is $400. ABC will beat this price by 10% so they will refund $100 + 10 = $110.

29. C
The purpose of this passage is to persuade.

30. B
The correct answer can be found in the fourth sentence of the first paragraph.

Choice A is incorrect because repenting begins the day AFTER Mardi Gras. Choice C is incorrect because you can celebrate Mardi Gras without being a member of a Krewe.

Choice D is incorrect because exploration does not play any role in a modern Mardi Gras celebration.

31. B
Heinous: adj. shocking, terrible or wicked.

32. A
Harbinger: n. a person of thing that tells or announces the coming of someone or something

33. B
Judicious: Having, or characterized by, good judgment or sound thinking.

34. B
Ethanol: n. a colorless volatile flammable liquid C_2H_6O.

35. A
Respiratory: adj. Of, relating to, or affecting respiration or the organs of respiration.

36. B
Inherent: Naturally a part or consequence of something.

37. A
Vapid: adj. tasteless or bland.

38. C
Waif: n. homeless child or stray.

39. D
Homologous: adj. similar or identical.

40. B
Obsolete: adj. no longer in use; gone into disuse; disused or neglected.

41. A
Rankle: v. To cause irritation or deep bitterness.

42. D
Reusable

43. C
Torpid: adj. Lazy, lethargic or apathetic.

44. A
Gregarious: adj. Describing one who enjoys being in crowds and socializing.

45. B
Mutation: n. a change or alteration.

46. C
Lithe: adj. flexible or pliant.

47. A
Resent: v. to express displeasure or indignation.

48. A
Immaterial: irrelevant not having substance or matter.

49. A
Impeccable: adj. perfect, no faults or errors.

50. B
Pudgy: adj. fat, plump or overweight.

ENGLISH

1. C
The semicolon is used in a list where the list items have internal punctuation, such as "Key West, Florida."

2. C
The semicolon links independent clauses. An independent clause can form a complete sentence by itself.

3. A
The semicolon links independent clauses with a conjunction (However).

4. B
The sentence is correct. The semicolon links independent clauses. An independent clause can form a complete sentence by itself.

5. B
Double negative sentence. In double negative sentences, one negatives is replaced with "any."

6. A
The third conditional is used for talking about an unreal situation (that did not happen) in the past. For example, "If I had studied harder, [if clause] I would have passed the exam [main clause]. Which is the same as, "I failed the exam, because I didn't study hard enough."

7. D
Present perfect. You cannot use the Present Perfect with specific time expressions such as: yesterday, one year ago, last week, when I was a child, at that moment, that day, one day, etc. The Present Perfect is used with unspecific expressions such as: ever, never, once, many times, several times, before, so far, already, yet, etc.

8. C
Bring vs. Take. Usage depends on your location. Something coming your way is brought to you. Something going away is taken from you.

9. A
The sentence is correct. Went vs. Gone. Went is the simple past tense. Gone is used in the past perfect.

10. B
Fewer vs. Less. 'Fewer' is used with countables and 'less' is used with uncountables.

11. D
Its vs. It's. 'It's' is a contraction for it is or it has. 'Its' is a possessive pronoun meaning, more or less, of 'it,' or belonging to 'it.'

12. D
When using 'however,' place a comma before and after.

13. B
"Who" is the best choice because the sentence refers to a person.

14. A
Past perfect is the correct form because it refers to something that happened in the past (he was the greatest inventor) and is still true today.

15. C
The superlative "hottest" is used when expressing the highest degree, or a degree greater than that of anything it is compared with.

16. D
When comparing two, use 'the taller.' When comparing more than two, use 'the tallest.'

17. B
Here the word "sale" is used as a "word" and not as a word in the sentence, so quotation marks are used.

18. C
His father is a poet and a novelist. It is necessary to use 'a' twice in this sentence for the two distinct things.

19. C
Titles of short stories are enclosed in quotation marks, and commas always go inside quotation marks.

20. B
Present tense, "ran well" is correct. "Ran good" is never correct.

21. D
Punctuation always goes inside quotation marks.

22. D
Healthful vs. Healthy. 'Healthy' is used to describe something that is of good for your health and 'healthful' refers to habits or types.

23. A
In vs. Into. 'In' a room means inside. 'Into' refers to movement or action.

24. C
Lay vs. Lie. Lie requires an object and lay does not. So you can lie down, (no object. and you lay a book on the floor.

25. A
The third conditional is used for talking about an unreal situation (that did not happen) in the past. For example, "If I had studied harder, [if clause] I would have passed the exam [main clause]. Which is the same as, "I failed the exam, because I didn't study hard enough."

26. A
Learn vs. Teach. Learning is what students do, and teaching is what teachers do.

27. B
Lose vs. Loose. Lose is to no longer have, or to lose a race. Loose is not tied or able to move freely.

28. D
Persecute vs. Prosecute. To prosecute is to have a legal claim against someone and to persecute is to harass.

29. A
Precede vs. Proceed. To precede is to go first or in front of. To proceed is to go forward.

30. A
Quoted speech is not capitalized.

31. A
The sentence is correct. Periods and events are capitalized but not century numbers.

32. C
Brand names are capitalized.

33. B
Generic terms such as 'french fries' are not capitalized. Brand names are capitalized.

34. C
The names of sports teams, as proper nouns, are capitalized. In this sentence, the full name is capitalized, Blue Jays.

35. A
The sentence is correct. North, South, East, and West when used as sections of the country, but not as compass directions.

MATHEMATICS

1. A
2 + a number divided by 7.
(2 + X) divided by 7.
(2 + X)/7

2. B
Total Volume = Volume of large cylinder - Volume of small cylinder

Volume of a cylinder = area of base • height = $\pi r^2 \cdot h$

Total Volume = (π * 12^2 * 10) - (π * 6^2 * 5) = 1440π - 180π

= 1260π in^3

3. C
1 hour is equal to 3,600 seconds and 1 kilometer is equal to 1000 meters.

Since this train travels 72 kilometers per hour, this means that it covers 72,000 meters in 3,600 seconds.

If it travels 72,000 meters in 3,600 seconds

It travels x meters in 12 seconds

By cross multiplication: x = 72,000 • 12 / 3,600

x = 240 meters

4. A
Let us first mention the money Tony spent: $80

Now we need to find the money Tony earned:

He had 15 dozen eggs = 15 * 12 = 180 eggs. 16 eggs were broken. So,

Remaining number of eggs that Tony sold = 180 − 16 = 164.

Total amount he earned for selling 164 eggs = 164 * 0.54 = $88.56.

As a summary, he spent $80 and earned $88.56.

The profit is the difference: 88.56 - 80 = $8.56

Percentage profit is found by proportioning the profit to the money he spent:

8.56•100/80 = 10.7%

Checking the answers, we round 10.7 to the nearest whole number: 11%

5. A
If we know the coordinates of two points on a line, we can find the slope (m) with the below formula:

$m = (y_2 - y_1)/(x_2 - x_1)$ where (x_1, y_1) represent the coordinates of one point and (x_2, y_2) the other.

In this question:

(-9, 6) : $x_1 = -9$, $y_1 = 6$

(18, -18) : $x_2 = 18$, $y_2 = -18$

Inserting these values into the formula:

m = (-18 - 6)/(18 - (-9)) = (-24)/(27) ... Simplifying by 3:

m = -8/9

6. B
Number of absent students = 83 − 72 = 11

Percentage of absent students is found by proportioning the number of absent students to total number of students in the class = (11 * 100)/83 = 13.25

Checking the answers, we round 13.25 to the nearest whole number: 13%

7. B
$ab^2 (9+8) = 17ab^2$

8. B

Total expense is $2000 and we are informed that $5 is spent per meter. Combining these two information, we know that the total length of the fence is 2000/5 = 400 meters.

The fence is built around a square-shaped field. If one side of the square is "a," the perimeter of the square is "4a." Here, the perimeter is equal to 400 meters. So,

400 = 4a

100 = a → this means that one side of the square is equal to 100 meters

9. A

If we know the coordinates of two points on a line, we can find the slope (m) with the below formula:
m = $(y_2 - y_1)/(x_2 - x_1)$ where (x_1, y_1) represent the coordinates of one point and (x_2, y_2) the other.

In this question:

$(-4, y_1)$: x_1 = -4, y_1 = we will find

$(-8, 7)$: x_2 = -8, y_2 = 7

m = -7/4

Inserting these values into the formula:

-7/4 = $(7 - y_1)/(-8 - (-4))$

-7/4 = $(7 - y_1)/(-8 + 4)$

7/(-4) = $(7 - y_1)/(-4)$ ... Simplifying the denominators of both sides by -4:

7 = 7 - y_1

0 = -y_1

y_1 = 0

10. D

To find the total turnout in all three polling stations, we need to proportion the number of voters to the number of all registered voters.
Total number of voters = 945 + 860 + 1210 = 3015

Total number of registered voters = 1270 + 1050 + 1440 = 3760

Percentage turnout in all three polling stations = 3015•100/3760 = 80.19%

Check the answer, round 80.19 to the nearest whole number: 80%

11. D
Area of Type B consists of two rectangles and a half circle. We can find these three areas and sum them up to find the total area:

Area of the left rectangle: (4 + 8)•8 = 96 m^2

Area of the right rectangle: 14•8 = 112 m^2

The diameter of the circle is equal to 14 m. So, the radius is 14/2 = 7:

Area of the half circle = (1/2)•π r^2 = (1/2)•(22/7)•(7)^2 = (1•22•49)/(2•7) = 77 m^2

Area of Type B = 96 + 112 + 77 = 285 m^2

Converting this area to ft^2: 285 m^2 = 285•10.76 ft^2 = 3066.6 ft^2

Type B is (3066.6 - 1300 = 1766.6 ft^2) 1766.6 ft^2 larger than type A.

12. B
Based on this graph, a person that is 85 will make 31.3 visits to the hospital every year.

13. A
Based on this graph, the number of visits per year is going up as age goes up, so we can expect a person that is 95 to have more than 31.3 visits to the hospital each year.

14. A
The formula of the volume of cylinder is the base area multiplied by the height. As the formula:

Volume of a cylinder = π r^{2}h. Where π is 3.142, r is radius of the cross sectional area, and h is the height.

We know that the diameter is 5 meters, so the radius is 5/2 = 2.5 meters.

The volume is: V = 3.142 * 2.5² * 12 = 235.65 m³.

15. C
The large cube is made up of 8 smaller cubes with 5 cm sides. The volume of a cube is found by the third power of the length of one side.

Volume of the large cube = Volume of the small cube•8

= (5³)•8 = 125•8

= 1000 cm³

There is another solution for this question. Find the side length of the large cube. There are two cubes rows with 5 cm length for each. So, one side of the large cube is 10 cm.

The volume of this large cube is equal to 10³ = 1000 cm³

16. A
The line is pointing towards numbers greater than 2. The equation is therefore, X > 2.

17. C
Pythagorean Theorem:
(Hypotenuse)² = (Perpendicular)² + (Base)²
h² = a² + b²

Given: a = 6, h = 10
h² = a² + b²
b² = h² - a²
b² = 10² + 6²
b² = 100 – 36
b² = 64
b = 8

18. A
60/x = 75/100
60* 100/X = 75
6000/75 = X
X = 80

19. D
Two parallel lines intersected by a third line with angles of 75°
x = 75° (corresponding angles)
x + y = 180° (supplementary angles)
y = 180° - 75°
y = 105°

20. C
71 ÷ 1000 = 0.071.

21. A
.33 × .59 = .1947

22. D
Two parallel lines (m & side AB) intersected by side AC. This means that 50° and a angles are interior angles. So:
a = 50° (interior angles).

23. A
Collect like terms, 7x = 47 + 9 = 56,
divide both sides by 7
x = 8

24. C
The ten thousandths place in 1.7389 will be the 4th decimal place, 9.

25. A
.87 - .48 = 0.39.

26. C
Forty nine thousandths will place the '9' in the 3rd decimal place, 0.049.

27. C
a. 3/4 * 2/2 = 6/8
b. 3/4 * 3/3 = 9/12
c. 3/4 * 4/4 = 12/18 – Incorrect!

28. A
    a. 84/231 = 12/33 > 1/3
    b. 6/35 = 1/5 < 1/3
    c. 3/22 = 1/7 < 1/3

29. C
Here are the choices:
a. 1
b. $\sqrt{2}$ = 1.414
c. 3/2 = 1.5   Largest number
d. 4/3 = 1.33

30. B
Collecting similar terms (algebraic addition).
2b + 9b − 5b = 11b - 5b = 6b

31. D
Remove parenthesis
$4Y^3 - 2Y^2 + 7Y^2 + 3Y - Y$
add and subtract like terms, $4Y^3 + 5Y^2 + 2Y$

32. C
4.7 + .9 + .01 = 5.61.

33. D
Open parenthesis, (7 x 2y + 7 x 8) + 1- (4 x y -20) =
14y + 56 + 1 - 4y - 20,
Collect like terms =14y -4y + 56 + 1 − 20 = 10y + 37

34. D
The distance between two points is found by
= $[(x_2 - x_1)^2+(y_2 - y_1)^2]^{1/2}$

In this question:

(18, 12) : x_1 = 18, y_1 = 12

(9, -6) : x_2 = 9, y_2 = -6

Distance= $[(9 - 18)^2 + (-6 - 12)^2]^{1/2}$

= $[(-9)^2 + (-18)^2]^{1/2}$

= $(9^2 + 2^2 \cdot 9^2)^{1/2}$

= $(9^2(1 + 5))^{1/2}$ ... We can take 9 out of the square root:

= $9 * 6^{1/2}$

= $9\sqrt{6}$

= 9 * 2.45

= 22.04

The distance is about 22 units.

35. D
60% of x = 12

(60/100)x = 12

60x = 1200

x = 20

36. D
.84/.7 = 1.2

37. C
6x - 24 = 3x + 12
6x - 3x = 12 + 24
3x = 36
x = 12

38. D
We have a circle given with diameter 8 cm and a square located within the circle. We are asked to find the area of the circle for which we only need to know the length of the radius that is the half of the diameter.
Area of circle = πr^2 ... r = 8/2 = 4 cm

Area of circle = $\pi * 4^2$

= 16π cm² ... As we notice, the inner square has no role in
this question.

39. B
Perimeter of a parallelogram is the sum of the sides.
Perimeter = 2(l + b)
Perimeter = 2(3 +10), 2 x 13
Perimeter = 26 cm.

40. D
He pays 'ns' amount to the employees for 7 days. The 'x' amount will be for '7x/ns' days.

41. C
Converting a percentage to a decimal – divide the numerator by the denominator.
87 ÷ 100 = 0.87.

42. C
Volume of a cylinder is π x r^2 x h
Diameter = 5 ft. so radius is 2.5 ft.
Volume of cylinder= π x 2.5^2 x 2
= π x 6.25 x 2 = 12.5 π
Approximate π to 3.142
Volume of the cylinder = 39.25

Volume of a rectangle = height X width X length.
= 5 X 5 X 4 = 100

Total volume = Volume of rectangular solid + volume of cylinder
Total volume = 100 + 39.25
Total volume = 139.25 ft^3 or about 140 ft^3

43. D
The jacket costs $545.00 so we can round up to $550. 10% of $550 is 55. We can round down to $50, which is easier to work with. $550 - $50 is $500. The jacket will cost about $500.

The actual cost will be 10% X 545 = $54.50
545 – 54.50 = $490.50

44. A
Five greater than 3 times a number.
5 + 3 times a number.
5 + 3X

45. B
If we know the coordinates of two points on a line, we can find the slope (m) with the below formula:
$m = (y_2 - y_1)/(x_2 - x_1)$ where (x_1, y_1) represent the coordinates

of one point and (x_2, y_2) the other.

In this question:

(-4, -4) : $x_1 = -4$, $y_1 = -4$

(-1, 2) : $x_2 = -1$, $y_2 = 2$

Inserting these values into the formula:

m = (2 - (-4))/(-1 - (-4)) = (2 + 4)/(-1 + 4) = 6/3 ... Simplifying by 3:

m = 2

46. C
Pythagorean Theorem:
(Hypotenuse)² = (Perpendicular)² + (Base)²
$h^2 = a^2 + b^2$

Given: $3^2 + 4^2 = h^2$
$h^2 = 9 + 16$
h = √25
h = 5

47. D
First calculate total square feet, which is 15 X 24 = 360 sq. ft. Next convert to square yards, (1sq. ft. = 0.1111 sq. yards) which is 360 X 0.1111 = 39.9999 or 40 square yards. At $0.50 per square yard, the total cost is $20.

48. B
Flat Screen TVs are the third best-selling product.

49. B
The two products that are closest in the number of sales, are Flat Screen TVs and Radar Detectors.

50. C
Comparing respective sides, ABCD, KLMN, WXYZ are similar.

CONCLUSION

Congratulations! You have made it this far because you have applied yourself diligently to practicing for the exam and no doubt improved your potential score considerably! Getting into a good school is a huge step in a journey that might be challenging at times but will be many times more rewarding and fulfilling. That is why being prepared is so important.

Study then Practice and then Succeed!

Good Luck!

Register for Free Updates and More Practice Test Questions

Register your purchase at
https://www.test-preparation.ca/register/
for updates, free test tips and more practice test questions.

Visit us Online

www.test-preparation.ca

Online Resources

How to Prepare for a Test - The Ultimate Guide

https://www.test-preparation.ca/the-ultimate-guide-to-test-preparation-strategy/

Learning Styles - The Complete Guide

https://www.test-preparation.ca/learning-styles/

Test Anxiety Secrets!

https://www.test-preparation.ca/how-to-overcome-test-anxiety/

Time Management on a Test

https://www.test-preparation.ca/test-tactics-the-time-wise-approach/

Flash Cards - The Complete Guide

https://www.test-preparation.ca/flash-cards/

Test Preparation Video Series

https://www.test-preparation.ca/video-series-on-test-preparation-multiple-choice-strategies-and-how-to-study/

How to Memorize - The Complete Guide

https://www.test-preparation.ca/memorize/